Praise for Stephen J.
21 Secrets of Million-l

"I've worked with successful financial advisors for decades and have partnered with all the industry's top presenters and thought leaders. No one is better than Steve Harvill when it comes to dynamically delivering actionable, executable, and intelligent content. His presentations and sales ideas make sense and are uncomplicated."

—Park Avenue Securities

"Steve will guide you on a journey that will show you how to hit the reset button for defining the 'Relevance' you can have in the lives of the customers you serve along with the 'Value' you can create that forms the lasting ties to those customers."

—First Clearing

"Steve inspires our teams to go beyond their comfort zones."

—JCPenney

"Steve's passion is contagious, his message is powerful, and his presentation is entertaining and enlightening."

—Better Business Bureau

"What Steve gave to us was so much more than consultation. His impact, without a doubt, is a lasting one that will reap rewards for our mission for years to come."

—American Heart Association

21
SECRETS
OF
MILLION-DOLLAR SELLERS

AMERICA'S TOP EARNERS REVEAL
THE KEYS TO SALES SUCCESS

Stephen J. Harvill

TOUCHSTONE

New York   London   Toronto   Sydney   New Delhi

Touchstone
An Imprint of Simon & Schuster, LLC
1230 Avenue of the Americas
New York, NY 10020

First Touchstone trade paperback edition August 2018

TOUCHSTONE and colophon are registered trademarks of Simon & Schuster, LLC.

The names and identifying details of some individuals in this book have been changed.

For information about special discounts for bulk purchases, please contact Simon & Schuster Special Sales at 1-866-506-1949 or business@simonandschuster.com.

The Simon & Schuster Speakers Bureau can bring authors to your live event. For more information or to book an event, contact the Simon & Schuster Speakers Bureau at 1-866-248-3049 or visit our website at www.simonspeakers.com.

Interior design by Jill Putorti

10 9 8 7 6 5 4

The Library of Congress has cataloged the hardcover edition as follows:

Names: Harvill, Stephen J., author.
Title: 21 secrets of million-dollar sellers : America's top earners reveal
  the keys to sales success / by Stephen J. Harvill.
Other titles: Twenty one secrets of million-dollar sellers
Description: New York : Touchstone, [2017] | Description based on print
  version record and CIP data provided by publisher; resource not viewed.
Identifiers: LCCN 2017009299 (print) | LCCN 2017022701 (ebook) | ISBN
  9781501153471 (Ebook) | ISBN 9781501153457 (hardcover) | ISBN 9781501153464 (pbk.)
Subjects: LCSH: Selling. | Sales personnel—United States. | Success in
  business—United States.
Classification: LCC HF5438.25 (ebook) | LCC HF5438.25 .H385 2017 (print)
  | DDC 658.85—dc23
LC record available at https://lccn.loc.gov/2017009299

ISBN 978-1-5011-5345-7
ISBN 978-1-5011-5346-4 (pbk)
ISBN 978-1-5011-5347-1 (ebook)

To Laura, who has always said,
"Babe, you can do anything"

CONTENTS

CONTENTS

— Part III —
WORK PERFORMANCE SECRETS
Harness Your Energy, Get Organized, and Manage Your Schedule Like a Sales Superstar

21
SECRETS
OF
MILLION-
DOLLAR
SELLERS

INTRODUCTION

If you make a living selling anything to anyone, this book is for you. If you are already good at your job, the tips in these pages will make you better. If you're great at your job, you may even rise to become one of the best.

But don't take my word for it. The advice here isn't stuff I made up. These 21 Secrets represent the real behaviors of some of the world's best salespeople, those who consistently generate a minimum of $1 million in sales a year for their companies. In sales jargon, this rare, elite professional is called a million-dollar producer—or even, in some cases, a multimillion-dollar producer.

THE MILLION-DOLLAR CLUB

For my survey, I spoke with a wide variety of top U.S.-based sales producers: wily veterans and young Turks; men and women; people from various regions and of various ethnicities. Since the entire study was based on merit, I didn't set out to find a broad cross-section of interviewees. I figured the mix of age, race, and gender would work itself out, and it did.

INTRODUCTION

Some quick statistics on the salespeople in my study:

○ They work for companies of all sizes; some are self-employed.

○ They (or they and their teams) bring in at least one million dollars' worth of business every year.

○ The biggest percentage works in finance or insurance, two industries with lots of salespeople and a wide range of products and services. The next largest percentage comes from the pharmaceutical industry, followed by real estate, automotive, advertising, and medical equipment.

○ About 75 percent are men and 25 percent are women, reflecting the demographics of the companies I worked with. (Women are more prevalent in real estate and pharmaceutical sales.)

○ About 70 percent are white (again reflecting the demographics of the companies I worked with); the remaining 30 percent are black, Latino, East Asian, or South Asian.

○ Most are middle-aged or older, as it takes some time to achieve the level of success I was looking for.

○ Their estimated annual compensation ranges from $300,000 to a million or more.

How do I know that million-dollar producers actually do these things? Because I asked them.

My name is Steve Harvill, and for more than thirty years, I have helped successful businesses do what they do better, smarter, more elegantly, and more imaginatively. Some of the world's best-known companies in technology, finance, health care, and other industries hire my consulting firm, Creative Ventures, to present educational programs at conferences and key meetings. The idea is to energize workers and improve their performance: We teach businesspeople how to differentiate themselves from the competition by harnessing the power of story and by thinking creatively. Companies also hire us to come in, study how they do business, and improve their performance. They enlist us to simplify processes that have become unwieldy and to make their teams more effective. We help design and implement corporate strategies for sales forces and other departments of some of the biggest organizations in the world. Microsoft, AT&T, Frito-Lay, American Express, and Southwest Airlines are some of the corporations we have worked with over the years.

For a few years now, I also have been teaching corporate sales forces the secrets you'll find in this book. These behaviors help salespeople do better in every aspect of their job, from wooing new customers to keeping regular customers happy to managing daily tasks. The 21 secrets of million-dollar sellers hit at the heart of every company's lifeline: its sales process. Over a dozen of the biggest and most respected companies now use some or all of the 21 Secrets in their regular sales-training programs, and I have taught these secrets as part of business curricula all over the world.

Creative Ventures' 21 Secrets program is the result of a project I embarked on a few years ago, after I got the idea to ask million-dollar salesmen and saleswomen how they achieved such stratospheric results. I spent more than a year personally interviewing 175 sales superstars in seven different industries and learned that top performers don't fit any mold. They are introverts and extroverts. Some come off as go-getters; others as more laid-back. Certain personalities seem adept at the quick sale, while others thrive on the slow burn of a complex transaction. While some people do seem to be more naturally suited to the job than others, I have concluded that nature isn't everything. *What these top earners all have in common is what they do to be successful.* Consistent, steady action is the universal trait among everyone I interviewed.

So, if you weren't born with natural charisma, persistence, people skills, and thick skin, don't worry. Top earners more than make up for any deficiencies they might have by practicing every day what it takes to do the job. Action makes the difference between those who *think* they should be the best and those who *are* the best. These behaviors can be replicated by anyone. Including you.

HOW IT BEGAN

My obsession with the behaviors of million-dollar salespeople started when a Fortune 500 pharmaceutical firm contacted me to ask if I'd help survey its global sales force about their process and practices. Was I interested in this assignment?

Ah . . . yes!

Saying yes so fast turned out to be a mistake. By engaging my mouth ahead of my brain, I violated one of my own cardinal rules of business: Speed should never outweigh thought. (For million-dollar producers' interpretation of this idea, see Secret #13, Not So Fast.)

I didn't ask a single question about the survey the firm was conducting—the methodology, the hoped-for outcome, anything. It was such an honor to be asked to participate in a project for this gigantic international company that the only thing I wanted to know was: *When do you need me there?* With my sketchbook in hand, I kissed my wife good-bye and set out from our home in Austin, Texas, to the client's New York headquarters.

ABOUT THAT SKETCHBOOK

Some people think in words. Some think in numbers. I think in images. When I'm brainstorming new ideas, I draw constantly on a pad, scratch paper, or whiteboard. By the time my associates and I are done planning a program or talking through a project, we have generated hundreds of cartoons, stick figures, arrows, symbols, and diagrams. I often counsel my clients to try this "sketchnoting." The process creates visual links that can help you understand and remember things better.

I arrived at my client's Manhattan headquarters on a chilly December day. In a conference room with spectacular views of the city, I finally learned why they'd called me for assistance. To gain an edge over its competitors, the company was about to survey its 250 salespeople to find out how they worked. How did the sales force approach prospective customers? How did they retain established customers? How often and how well did they make use of the resources the company provided for them?

My new client hoped its survey would uncover information it could use to gain market advantage by eliminating techniques that didn't pay off and encouraging those that did. The pharmaceutical company had already hired an outside contractor to create the survey, which would soon be distributed to the sales teams. Once the answers were in, I was told, my job would be to review and analyze the data and draw conclusions about how to improve the sales force's future performance.

Then, in that conference room, they showed me the survey.

Here is what I wrote in my sketchbook: *YIKES*.

Even though I work in the business world, I studied science in college. In a different set of circumstances I might have ended up becoming a marine biologist. Thanks to that science training, I still try to approach problems the way scientists do: by observing, investigating, questioning the evidence, opening my mind, and sprinkling in the creative process of discovery.

The survey was the kind of questionnaire we have all seen at one time or another. It had obviously been developed with a lot of thought and consideration, but the questions were all closed-ended. Here are a couple of examples:

How often are you in contact with your elite clients?

- ☐ *Weekly*
- ☐ *Bimonthly*
- ☐ *Monthly*
- ☐ *Quarterly*
- ☐ *Biannually*
- ☐ *Annually*

How often do you access the sales intranet?

☐   *Daily*

☐   *Weekly*

☐   *Monthly*

My first question for the company that had hired me was whether the survey could also include some open-ended questions so the salespeople could provide some subjective answers—their own opinions and thoughts on what worked and what didn't. But I was told that the sheer size of the survey group would make that impossible. I sensed an immediate problem. This questionnaire didn't ask anything that would reveal significant insight about sales behavior. To get sales insights they would truly be able to use, the corporation should have commissioned an in-depth, subjective study in which salespeople could describe their specific behaviors. Subjective studies are time-consuming and expensive, though, so corporations often try to replace them with objective, data-driven studies that provide plenty of metrics but little usable information. (For more on the limitations of objective data, see Secret #17, Make Your Own Metrics.)

I wasn't sure what helpful conclusions I would be able to draw from the results, but it was clear that the company was already well on the road to conducting the study as designed. I was along for the ride.

Meanwhile, I got a second phone call. About a month after I began this sales-force questionnaire assignment, my largest regular client, an insurance firm, invited me to its national sales meeting. Over the years I had consulted with this mega-corporation in a number of areas. I helped its sales teams with skills training, strategic planning, and goal setting. For this assignment, I was to attend as many of the sessions and programs as possible during its multiple-day national sales shindig, after which I'd provide input on what worked well, what was horrible, and whether the entire event had had any real value for the sales force.

This time, I jumped on a flight to—where else?—Las Vegas, the Mount Olympus of sales meetings.

My insurance client is good at meetings, and over the years I had helped create some of its events. This year I was simply hanging out. I went to workshops, regional gatherings, strategy sessions, and all the social stuff. Then came the crowning event: the National Sales Awards Dinner.

Yeah, you guessed it: large ballroom, pre-plated salad and dessert, cold dinner rolls and rock-hard butter, a glitzy stage with an awards table full of crystal things and a lectern smack-dab in the middle. Awards were given for goals met, goals exceeded, and top performances in a wide variety of categories. People received crystal things and wooden things. Some got bonuses. All of them got their photos taken.

Then came the Moment. The highlight of the evening was the award for National Salesperson of the Year. After much fanfare, a name was announced—"Mary!"—and a woman from across the room stood up to thunderous applause and made the famous Academy Awards walk to the stage. Mary was given the biggest crystal thing and then a check—one of those huge Tiger Woods display checks that take multiple people to hold up.

The number on the check nearly knocked me out of my seat.

I turned to the guy sitting next to me. "How did she earn that?" I asked.

"She sold more than anyone in the company," he said.

Duh. I'd figured that part out. "No, really," I said. "What did she *do* that made her the top seller?"

No one at my table could answer that question.

THE PROJECT

On my flight home, I was struck by the fact that my work with two different clients had left me with two related observations. I didn't believe my new pharmaceutical client's sales-force questionnaire would yield the results the company was looking for. The company wouldn't discover what made its sales teams successful or unsuccessful without probing into what the salespeople were *really* doing and thinking. The survey, as it stood, would reveal trends, perhaps, but nothing meaningful. Then there was the insurance client's national sales meeting. No one there seemed to have a clue about what their top performer, their Salesperson of the Year, had done to make herself so successful.

I was dying to know both of these things! During that two-hour flight, I began to sketch out a plan to discover what I believed to be very important to every company's success.

By the time the plane touched down, I had a project outline. First, I wanted to interview super-successful producers—as many of them as I could. Second, I wanted to ask only open-ended questions, so interviewees could tell me stories that would uncover their true behaviors. Finally, the focus wouldn't be on a single industry. I wanted sales professionals selling a mix of products and services at companies with different cultures.

I suspected that across all industries, no matter what they sold, great sales producers shared many of the same behaviors and practices. I had seen more than a few of these behaviors in action over the course of my career working with sales teams and helping them develop their strategies. My hypothesis was that the study would uncover, identify, and classify specific actions anyone could replicate. I designed a study that would seek to learn exactly how top salespeople achieved their extraordinary outcomes.

To start, I picked five companies I already worked with, representing five robust industries large enough to supply me with a hefty sample of super-successful producers:

- Financial services
- Insurance (I eventually enlisted the company whose national sales meeting I'd attended.)
- Advertising and marketing
- Medical equipment
- Pharmaceuticals

Because a good study isn't static, after Creative Ventures began to work extensively with two more industries that fit the bill, I added them to the study, too. Both of these also include a lot of super-successful producers. As a bonus, while some of the other fields are heavily populated with male salespeople, real estate in particular includes a lot of women.

- Real estate
- Automobiles

NDA ALL THE WAY

When I began my research, I signed nondisclosure agreements and promised not to identify any company or its salespeople. The names in this book are pseudonyms, and I have changed some identifying details. (Because I never planned for this study to be a book, I didn't transcribe interviews word for word, so I've reconstructed some of the conversations from memory.) Most companies are extremely proprietary of their sales processes and wanted to protect them within the context of my study. But the companies are real (you've definitely heard of most of them). So are the people, and so are their behaviors.

I then asked each firm if I could talk to their elite salespeople. In return for the access, I'd give each company in the study the results of the survey free of charge.

What a deal, right?

Well, not so much. Almost every company said no.

Huh? Why not?

To my surprise, all but one organization—the insurance company—thought that their top producers' sales processes and behaviors were *secrets*. These secrets were so unique and powerful, my clients explained, that their release to the uneducated and unprofessional hordes would harm the company's market position.

What? Really? The fact is, the traditional idea of sales—exchanging money for goods—has been around since the Romans introduced currency in about 200 BC. "Do you honestly think that anything is a real and true secret?" I asked my contacts. "Wouldn't it be incredibly valuable for you and your sales force to know what works and what doesn't? Wouldn't you like to know which sales practices are so powerful that they cross industry lines—and that, no matter what they sell, the best of the best are doing these specific things?"

"Well, when you put it that way . . ." they said.

I eventually got approval from everyone. The study was a go.

The initial study took about fourteen months and involved trips all across the country, plus additional months of input from my Creative Ventures staff, who helped me sift through mountains of research to find the behavior patterns that turned into the 21 Secrets. Since then, I have continued to expand the research and regularly update the study with additional superstar salespeople whenever I find them. I occasionally add outliers from new industries—from mom-and-pop investment firms to one guy who has found sweet success selling pies. I personally interview each salesperson, including the original 175 men and women in the study. (One of them was Mary, my insurance client's Salesperson of the Year, by the way.)

I ask each person the same ten questions to spur an in-depth discussion about their behaviors:

The Questions

1. **Tell me about your key skills.** Which do you think are directly related to your success? How often do you build on your skills through continuing education?
2. **Tell me about your product and industry knowledge.** How much do you know about what you sell, and how does that connect to your success?
3. **Tell me how you manage your day.** What tasks do you focus on in order to reach your sales goals?
4. **Tell me how you use your support staff.** How do your team members contribute to your success?
5. **Tell me how you build relationships with current clients.** How do you connect with them outside of the business transaction?
6. **Tell me how you get new clients.** How do you build your book of business? Do you find new prospects through referrals from existing clients or by some other method?
7. **Tell me how you plan.** How do you prepare to meet your sales goals tomorrow, next week, and next year?
8. **Tell me how you set goals.** Do you decide on them, or does your company do it for you?
9. **Tell me about the metrics that matter to you.** Which benchmarks, quotas, and statistics are helpful and which aren't?
10. **Tell me your biggest roadblocks to success.** What, if anything, keeps you from making a sale?

Although these are all open-ended questions, I did build in some restraints. My interviewees could answer any way they wanted to as long as they did not ramble beyond the very specific topic I was asking about. If they did, I gently reeled them back in. Keeping these interviews focused was instrumental. It's how we discovered the patterns we were searching for.

TELL ME

To discover shared behaviors, habits, and attitudes that lead to sales success, we used an age-old process, a modified Socratic method: Keep the questions straightforward and start each one with "Tell me . . ." When you use the "Tell me" technique, every response you receive will be a story, and stories were what I was looking for. It is through stories, not 1-to-10 scales or true-false binaries, that people reveal details and specific behaviors.

Respondents can answer a "Tell me" question any way they wish as long as the answer fits within the confines of the question. Most big-time salespeople love to talk, especially about themselves, so I used a technique I called "creative restriction." I would allow the salespeople to talk as much and as long as they wanted to about the question on the table, but if they veered astray, I would stop them and bring them back to the question. It took a lot of concentration to make sure my interviewees stayed on message.

Since the study, Creative Ventures has become expert in this method of gathering information, and we have had the honor of applying it to many client projects.

Along with the sellers, I also talked to some of their clients—an idea I lit on much later in the study, when I met a saleswoman named Kat who regularly asks her customers what they like about doing business with her. (You'll hear about her in Secret #6, Build Your "Like" Platform.) It wasn't easy to persuade these salespeople to connect me with their best clients, but I was able to speak with about two dozen. What do these hotshots' customers appreciate about their sales approach? The customers' answers provided valuable input for the final list of 21 Secrets.

By the way, remember what I said a few pages ago about how no sales strategy is truly a secret? I still believe that. Some of the behaviors and strategies you'll read about in this book will be new to you. Some may sound familiar. But none of this stuff is truly *secret*. That said, it turns out that the word "secret" sells books. So that's why this book, and the knowledge within, is called *21 Secrets*.

HOW LONG WILL THIS TAKE?

My interviewees are busy folks. Most are very typical type A personalities, and a lot of times when I spoke with them they fidgeted like they had somewhere else to be—no doubt out selling. They all wanted to know, "How long is this interview going to take?" I'd say, truthfully, that I was not sure but would do everything in my power not to keep them too long.

Early in the study, I interviewed a guy named Gordon who works in financial services. (His boss told him he had to speak to me; I'm guessing he wouldn't have been there otherwise.) Before I met him, I was warned, "This guy is never going to sit and share information with you. He can't go five minutes without looking at his phone."

With that in mind, before I started the interview I asked Gordon, "How often do you really need to check your phone?" After some discussion, we settled on a time frame, and I set a timer to let Gordon have a phone fix every fifteen minutes. He turned out to be one of my most enlightening interviews. You'll find some of his wisdom in later chapters.

Many months later, when I finished up the last interview and again was on a plane home—this time from Chicago—I began wondering how in the world I would make sense of all these stories. I had tape after tape of recorded answers and stacks of filled notebooks.

The solution was pretty old-school. With flip charts and whiteboards, office windows (which make excellent drawing surfaces) and huge rolls of butcher paper, my associates and I began mining all of these interviews for common themes. It wasn't long until every square inch of wall, floor, and window space in the Creative Ventures office in Dallas was covered and patterns began to emerge.

When we started to recognize answers that seemed similar to those we'd read in other interviews, we moved these answers to the same space in the conference room. While interviewees described their behaviors using different analogies and metaphors, they were often saying essentially the same thing. I like to use a crayon analogy: Open a big box of crayons and you'll find all the variations of one color grouped together. Periwinkle, aqua, and midnight are next to each other. They're each different, but they're all "blue." Once we started grouping ideas together, we started to see common themes everywhere and the study started to make sense.

Now, this all may seem like a primitive way to sort information compared with the pattern-recognition algorithms out there that can comb through massive data dumps. But fancy computing and Big Data are only as good as what you can do with the information you get. Without creative insight, those numbers are just numbers.

The analysis yielded twenty-one distinct behaviors—twenty-one things these sales stars do that set them apart from the pack. Each interviewee expressed them differently, but all of these behaviors are part of everyone's routine. What struck me about the 21 Secrets was that these were things anyone could do. There is nothing proprietary or magical about them, but they make a difference when consciously applied over and over again.

It was not my original intention to turn this study into a book. I embarked on my research planning to design, in the Creative Ventures vernacular, a strategic platform. I would present and teach the sales behaviors to my own clients and consult with them on applying the behaviors to their sales practices. That's what did happen; in fact, the ideas that are now in this book have become the single most popular and profitable program in the three-decade history of my consultancy. For years, clients and salespeople would ask me, "Is there a book to go with this strategy?" And I would tell them no. I simply hadn't approached the study the way I might have approached it if I had planned to author a book. But here it is.

There's a point I want to make before we jump in: The underlying theme to every one of the 21 Secrets is *discipline*. To paraphrase Calvin Coolidge, nothing—not charisma, not talent, not innate intelligence—can replace persistence and dedication. Each and every participant in this study exhibited tremendous focus and self-control. These rock stars don't mess around, they don't procrastinate, and they don't make excuses. They attend to their careers with purpose.

It is impossible to separate "discipline" as a singular element in this study when it runs through each and every one of these behaviors.

So keep that in mind as you read the 21 Secrets. They don't work unless you *do* them.

One more thing you'll notice: The vast majority of the salespeople in the million-dollar club deal in products or services that are of high value, cost a lot, and are often business-to-business (not business-to-consumer) transactions. There are no toaster or chain saw salespeople in this study. That makes sense if you think about it: The margin for profit per chain saw is kind of small, and chain saws last a long time. If you are the neighborhood chain saw salesman, you'd have to sell a chain saw to everyone you ever met, whether that person needed one or not, to become a chain saw million-dollar producer. You just plain couldn't do it.

But if you move up to corporate chain saw sales and start selling truckloads of them to Lowe's and the Home Depot, you might score yourself a seat at the million-dollar sales table.

This doesn't mean that if you are new to the sales game, or if you deal in less expensive or lower-volume goods or services, you can't benefit and learn from the secrets in this book. Even though you may not be able to apply all 21 Secrets to your current career, you can use many of them to move up to the level at which you can. Remember: Every one of the million-dollar producers in this book started off *not* being a million-dollar producer.

Even if you're not officially "in sales," you can apply the 21 Secrets to your career or business. After all, there's an element of sales in almost every line of work, whether you're an independent contractor bidding for jobs, a small-business owner looking to improve your customer relationships, or a cubicle dweller trying to market yourself as worthy of a promotion.

Are you ready? Here we go.

— *Part I* —

The Four Essential Secrets

Universal Behaviors of Million-Dollar Salespeople

ESSENTIAL SECRET #1
SIMPLE

It gets cold in Portland, Maine. I mean *really cold*. I was there to speak with Joan, who seemed unfazed by the arctic conditions outside her office window. She even took me to the L.L.Bean flagship store in Portland to buy a bunch of warm clothes after the airline lost my luggage.

Joan is in commercial insurance sales. She specializes in what her industry calls CAT coverage. CAT stands for "catastrophic." So, if you own a hotel on the Gulf Coast and it seems to you that hurricane insurance would be a good idea, you track down Joan. Or, more likely, Joan already knows about you and has tracked *you* down.

Joan and I were chatting about the various ways good sales professionals can be of service to clients; in sales lingo, this is called "adding value." Joan offered up that there was one key way in which she made herself indispensable to her customers.

What was that? I asked.

She said, "I make things simple."

The million-dollar salespeople I spoke to during the course of my research brought up a lot of behaviors during our interviews.

So did their clients. But there were four specific, very special behaviors that were mentioned by both groups—the salespeople and their customers. I call these the Four Essential Secrets. If you only make a few changes in your own sales practices, I recommend that you start with these four secrets. And the very first one is SIMPLE.

SIMPLE is the holy grail of sales.

The one philosophy that every salesperson I interviewed shares is the dedicated commitment to making things SIMPLE for their clients. **Essential Secret #1 is about getting rid of any obstacles that might keep customers from doing business with you. It's about making every interaction with you a breeze for your clients, even if doing so complicates things for you.**

When I asked Joan what she meant by "I make it simple," her answer made me shake my head.

She said, "I build barriers."

"*Build* barriers? Don't you mean *tear down* barriers?" I asked. I thought she'd misspoken.

"Nope," she responded confidently.

Clients buying CAT insurance, she explained, have to slog through a lot of paperwork. They're bombarded with data, rules, requirements, statistics, and risk-management strategies. The policies themselves can be zillions of pages long. "It is ridiculous, all the stuff my clients have to look at," Joan said. "I keep them from getting overwhelmed by too much information."

Joan makes her clients' lives SIMPLE by screening and managing the paperwork and information, separating out the important data and regulations clients need to be aware of and tossing the rest. Once a client has signed on to an insurance policy, Joan turns herself into a human shield between the client and this avalanche of information. Along with the bazillion-page policy, for example, she will also send a simplified one-page summary of its main points— she writes the summary herself—so that her clients need not read the original document if they don't want to. She also weeds through the extraneous e-mail or paper mail they don't want or need—the insurers' miscellaneous glossy brochures, marketing information, and other corporate fluff that would normally start coming to her new clients, cluttering up their in-boxes and complicating their lives. With her clients' permission, she has all of that stuff sent to her instead of to them. Then she filters through it like a sieve and sends each client only what he or she needs or wants to see.

Joan not only provides the CAT coverage clients need, she also saves them time and energy. In slowing that "incessant flow of stuff," she told me, she protects her clients' time, just as her product protects their property.

SIMPLE IS NOT EASY

I often hear "simple" used as a synonym of "easy." In actuality, "easy" means a lack of effort. "Simple" means a lack of complexity, and achieving that isn't always easy. If you saw the movie *Julie & Julia*, you can sum up the difference between "simple" and "easy" in two words: boeuf bourguignon.

There is a scene in which amateur chef Julie Powell tries to make this classic beef, red wine, and mushroom stew. The recipe takes countless steps, so many steps that Julie falls asleep in the middle of cooking it. Boeuf bourguignon is a "simple" comfort food that is not at all "easy" to pull off.

In sales, your goal is to make everything SIMPLE for your customers. Doing that may or may not be easy for you.

For Sonny, a luxury-automobile salesman, "simple" means "understandable." As he explained to me, when you help a client truly understand your product or service and what makes it different, special, and better, the client starts to trust you. The client engages. The client sees benefits. Most important, the client *buys*.

Unlike Joan, Sonny was basking in the Florida sunshine during our interview. Sonny and his team sold very cool cars—Jaguars and Land Rovers—and plenty of 'em, even though these are not everyday cars. The price of a new Jaguar starts at almost $55,000 and goes way up from there. A Land Rover will set you back as much as six figures. As Sonny said, "We are not in the car business; we are in the luxury business." And his task, as he saw it, was to communicate what "luxury" means.

WATCH AND LEARN

You'd think the process of buying a wristwatch would be pretty straightforward. I mean, watches really only need to do one thing: tell time. Yet shopping for a watch can mean struggling to absorb a mind-boggling list of features, from face size to bezel type to water resistance to internal movement to extras like tachymeters. (Yes, as the watch industry faces obsolescence, with more people relying on their cell phones for timekeeping, it is fighting back by *adding* complexity.)

If you're a watch seller, how do you help a buyer understand all of this without their eyes glazing over? One retailer, World of Watches, posts a ninety-second video on its website for many of its timepieces alongside the more standard list of features. The video quickly summarizes the watch's bells and whistles, demonstrates how it looks and fits on a wrist, and even suggests whether the watch is a good value for its price. Not surprisingly, the company says eight out of ten shoppers don't even bother reading the list of features. Instead, they make their buying decision based on the video. Watches may be getting more complicated, but this seller makes buying one SIMPLE.

A twenty-two-year sales veteran, Sonny was telling me the story of his SIMPLE breakthrough. Early on in his career, he said, "I discovered that language played a key role in sales." He realized that the more complicated his descriptions were of a car's features and benefits, the harder it was to close a deal. So Sonny decided to change the way he and his team spoke to car shoppers. "I simplified everything," he said. To describe a car's options, he deliberately stopped using the typical cold-and-clinical grandiose jargon you hear in automobile commercials. "We don't say 'ergonomic interior,'" Sonny told me. "We say, 'Jaguar designed this vehicle to be comfortable.' The car doesn't have a 'floating roofline'; it has a roof that appears to seamlessly attach to the auto's body, a design element that makes you recognize *this is a Jaguar* right away.

"Someone seriously considering a Jaguar or Land Rover is looking to make a personal statement," he continued. "The more I can simplify the language and make it more concrete to them and their personal commitment, the more likely they are to trust my descriptions. So I speak to them in a language they understand."

Starting to see a pattern? Both Joan and Sonny created simplicity for their clients. They view SIMPLE as a sales strategy and actively look for ways to simplify. Joan practices SIMPLE by reducing the amount of needless information bombarding her clients. Sonny used SIMPLE to communicate his cars' features using language that his customers could relate to. (Sonny is now retired, by the way. He took his bucketful of money and bought a boat and a nice place on the Intracoastal Waterway.)

SIMPLE varies from industry to industry and from sales professional to sales professional. The challenge for you is to figure out what specifically about your sales process can be simplified and make it happen.

REMOTE POSSIBILITIES

John Maeda, a former president of the Rhode Island School of Design, writes that one element of SIMPLE is "thoughtful reduction." This process of removing the extraneous and unnecessary, he says, is "the simplest way to simplicity."

Another way to say this: When in doubt, take it out.

But be careful. Removing something just for the sake of removing it can be a mistake. The key word is "thoughtful."

To help you get a handle on this idea, let's do an exercise:

Go get one of your many TV remote controls (you know you have a lot of them). While you're at it, grab a pen and a piece of paper.

Once you are looking at the remote . . . what do you notice? Probably: *Man, this thing has a lot of buttons.* As a matter of fact, the average television remote has forty-seven. Now guess how many the average television watcher uses? Seven of them, plus the number pad.

Now's the time to use your pen and paper. Take a few minutes and do a quick redesign of the remote buttons, streamlining and reducing them to make the remote SIMPLE. Which buttons would you eliminate, perhaps combining them with others or replacing with one big button?

Finished? Okay, first, I bet you removed the number pad. Maybe you replaced it with an iPhone-style circular "home" button. (Or maybe you went total voice command.) You're thinking you can make the remote SIMPLE by removing the numbers and just scrolling through the channels.

But is this a thoughtful reduction? If you're looking for something to watch on TV, you may regularly scroll through all the channels, but when you want to go directly to one of your favorite channels—Channel 1660, the Tennis Channel, for me—you don't scroll through everything else to get there. You just push 1-6-6-0. This is an almost universal behavior of remote users: They actually use the number buttons.

Yet, in this exercise, which I use all the time in my consulting work, the number buttons are often a feature people remove in their rush to reduce. Remember: *thoughtful* reduction. While you're making your sales process SIMPLE, think about the user: your client.

Now that you're sold on SIMPLE, let's apply it to *your* sales process. Here's how to start:

1. Make a master list. In sales, getting to SIMPLE starts with writing down every element of your sales process, with the eventual goal of making the whole process less complicated for your customers. (Again, not necessarily less complicated for you.)

So grab your team or do it solo; either way, you need to write down everything involved in selling, from staff meetings to client lunches.

Here's an example of the master list in action:

A small financial services company wanted to attract more new clients. They did a great job with their existing accounts, but when it came to adding new ones to the stable, they were struggling and couldn't figure out why.

The sales team's first step was to list everything they were currently doing to attract clients. The list looked like this:

a. We have a strong network of referrals from our current clients.

b. We host events for people who express an interest in our services.

c. We go to prospective clients' homes or offices for one-on-one meetings, sparing them the inconvenience of traveling to us.

... and so on.

2. Reorient. Once you have a list of every component of your sales process, it's time to shift perspectives. You created that list from your point of view. Now look at it from your clients' point of view. Start by ignoring any steps that don't directly involve them. If you are required to do a monthly internal sales report, for example, that is technically part of your sales process, but your clients never see it, so you don't need to worry about that right now.

Once you're left with only the steps that affect your clients—current clients, prospective clients, whatever—take a look at each step. As hard as it might be, think like your customers. Ask yourself, *Which of these steps might my customers view as an obstacle to doing business with me?*

You will almost certainly discover, as you look at the sales process through your clients' eyes, glaring opportunities to make it SIMPLE.

For Joan, the insurance saleswoman, one opportunity was to cut through all the paperwork and junk mail. For Sonny it was "un-complicate the language we use to convey luxury." Your own process no doubt has a few steps you can make SIMPLE for your clients' benefit. You can change these steps, streamline them, or delete them altogether.

3. Make it SIMPLE. Now you've reduced your list to only those steps that affect your customers, and you've considered how to streamline some steps to create value for your client. Let's make things easy, as in "requiring less effort," and pick one step to focus on. But which? Here's a suggestion: Choose one you can get going quickly, with relatively little trouble. (For more on this idea, check out Secret #5, One Level Above.) In the case of the small financial services company, by the way, they ultimately realized their sales process was pretty streamlined and that what they needed to work on was honing their sales story. There's more on story in Essential Secret #3, Tell a Good Tale.

CUTTING THE DECK

At Creative Ventures, every stage presentation we put on begins with what we call a "master deck." We capture every idea we have for the program in a slide, with images to illustrate each idea. By the time we're done, we have a huge, everything-but-the-kitchen-sink PowerPoint presentation that would probably take all day to deliver. But since we usually only have about ninety minutes, we use thoughtful reduction to edit down the deck. Reducing the master deck to only the slides we think are most important is a huge challenge.

Once we've done that, we reorient and view the presentation from our audience's perspective. We sit where the audience will sit and run through the slides, sharing our feelings about each one: Does this image illustrate the idea we're trying to get across? Will most of the viewers "get" it? And will the next part of the program take our audience from "I get it" to "I can do it"? If we have built that bridge, then we have a successful program.

SIMPLE is about making the process of buying as effortless as possible for your clients. Do SIMPLE well, and you'll separate and differentiate yourself from your competitors.

WHITE FLAG

It seems you can't talk about SIMPLE without mentioning Apple. Their elegant ingenuity is legendary. I could write all day about Apple's mastery of SIMPLE, but I will give you just one definitive example: white earbuds.

It was 2005. I had been at Apple's Silicon Valley headquarters to consult on the company's internal training program (now called Apple University) and had gone from there to San Francisco to meet with another client. Wandering down Market Street, I started noticing how many people had white wires running from their ears into their pockets. Those white in-ear headphones were *everywhere*! And each time I spotted a pair, I knew the wearer owned not just an MP3 player but, specifically, an Apple iPod.

Why? Apple had made the simple design decision—arrived at after months of consideration (remember, "simple" does not mean easy)—to make its product white instead of the standard black. So even if you couldn't see what brand of MP3 player each person had hidden away, the white earbuds, and only the white earbuds, immediately telegraphed "iPod." Which meant that every single iPod owner was also a walking iPod ad.

More than a decade later, even though Apple's earbuds are now wireless, they're still white.

How SIMPLE is that?

ESSENTIAL SECRET #2

The Jordan Formula

The Jordan Formula has to do with your commitment to your profession. It's about the effort you make behind the scenes in order to be a superstar. Nobody illustrates this better than NBA legend Michael Jordan, which is why Essential Secret #2 is named in his honor. MJ was obviously gifted with tremendous innate talent. But talent alone wasn't enough to make him, arguably, the greatest basketball player of all time. That took years of discipline, countless hours of practice, and thousands of bleary-eyed sessions studying game footage.

Million-dollar salespeople are the Michael Jordans of their profession.

I'm not going to sugarcoat this: This is a book about superstars—an elite, gifted subset of human beings. I would venture to say that superstars in any field enjoy a certain amount of natural acumen that most people are not lucky enough to be blessed with—and that natural talent definitely has a role in making them superstars. But it's not the only thing responsible for their success. The rest is hard work. Million-dollar producers understand that whatever gifts you might possess, you'll never be at the top of your game without preparation and sweat. **Innate talent + consistent, focused work over time = superstardom. That is the Jordan Formula.**

"I wasn't born a guitar player," Jack, a sales superstar I interviewed, told me. "In fact, I am mostly tone-deaf, but I made myself into a guitar player. I wasn't born a boat captain—I used to get seasick—but I made myself into a boat captain. I was not born a great salesman. I made myself into one."

Jack wasn't exaggerating; he is a sales maestro. A first-generation American born to Korean parents and fluent in both Korean and English, Jack has leveraged his familiarity with his cultural heritage to become the king of financial services in New York City's Koreatown, with a client base made up entirely of well-heeled immigrants. Jack is a cultural phenomenon, but he will quickly tell you how much effort he put in to make himself so.

Jack is an introvert. Quiet and professional, he lacks the innate bravado normally associated with great sales performers. He admitted, "It's hard for me to create the emotional momentum necessary to make a sale. It doesn't come naturally. Instead, I have to really work at it. And I work at it *all the time!*"

Jack has put in hours and hours and hours of practice to become more outgoing. From online video courses to Toastmasters, Jack spent his early years working on his game. "I was looking for confidence," he said. "I *needed* confidence—and the more I worked at it, the more I moved my professional needle forward." To this day he continues to practice his presentation and people skills.

"So it's all about working harder than the next guy . . ." he began, and then corrected himself. "No—it's about working harder on the right stuff, that kind of 'working smart' thing you hear about. I work harder and smarter. And I am brutally honest about my weaknesses and my strengths."

A visit to Jack's office reveals the rewards of his self-study and his effort: He has been named the top producer in his company twelve times and has a wall full of awards to prove it.

HOOPS HISTORY

I remember the March 28, 1990, Chicago at Cleveland game like it was yesterday. The Bulls, led by Michael Jordan, had been torching the Cavs all season, and Jordan started this game on fire. I had the sense that the night would be special and ran to wake up my sons, Dylan, then nine, and Colin, then six. School night or no school night, I was pretty sure they were about to witness a game that would go down in sports history.

I was right! Jordan went on to score a staggering 69 points and grab 18 rebounds, 6 assists, and 4 steals in that game. It was a career high for MJ; the Bulls went on to beat the Cavs in overtime. That game was the extraordinary result of talent plus hard work over time.

Million-dollar salespeople understand how much effort it takes to be good at what they do. More important, they actually *make* the effort. I know this advice seems obvious. But when I bring up the Jordan Formula during presentations, I often hear, "I know I *should* do this, but . . ." Meaning they *don't* do it.

Think about it: Why was MJ so great? Aside from his speed, power, and athleticism, he also had:

Confidence

A supreme command of his skills

A well-honed understanding of the competition

... all of which he developed through practice.

Just as basketball fans only see the game, not the practice, it's very likely none of their customers have any idea how hard million-dollar sales superstars work to excel. You can also think of Essential Secret #2 as the Iceberg Principle. If you've ever seen an iceberg (or, more likely, *Titanic*), you know that the part of the iceberg visible above the water is a very small piece of the entire thing. Almost the entire mass of an iceberg is hidden below the water. That metaphor definitely describes the performance of million-dollar producers. When a great producer closes yet another deal, that is the visible part of the iceberg. Underneath that success lies the tremendous discipline and endless hours of practice.

How diligently did my interviewees work at being superstars? *Very*.

For example, Antonio. I love Antonio. I interviewed him at a Rhode Island conference for people who sold financial products. Part of my love for Antonio came when, during a lull in the conference, he asked me if I wanted to go to the Tennis Hall of Fame!

He knew I was a tennis player. (I told him I would love to, but the Tennis Hall of Fame is in Newport, all the way across the state, and we were in Providence. He said, "So what? That's only thirty-four miles from here." The small size of East Coast states amazes me. You could drive for a couple of hours from somewhere in Dallas and *still* be in Dallas.) It was a once-in-a-lifetime experience I remember to this day, and it was exactly the sort of VIP treatment Antonio provides to his actual clients.

Antonio is a million-dollar producer with a wide range of expertise. His success stems from his breadth of knowledge about investments: Instead of specializing in a narrow, niche financial product, as many of his peers do, he takes a shotgun approach and has educated himself about such a wide variety of investments that he could, theoretically, meet any client's financial needs. He is so proficient that it took him less than five years to rise from fledgling salesperson to million-dollar superstar.

His success came at a cost, and that cost was time. Lots and lots of time. Antonio spends almost as much time studying investments as he does selling them. He just plain outworks many of his peers. To get and stay up to speed in his industry, he regularly comes in early and stays late to research the financial world. Early in his career, Antonio also made the effort to cultivate a network of professionals within his company. Now, when he doesn't know something about bond sales, annuities, or whatever, he can go to one of his experts for information.

Antonio's biggest advantage is not his inborn talent. It is that he makes the effort to "build my sales brain," as he described it. Antonio outworks, outlearns, and thus outsells his competitors.

Natural shine all by itself won't get you into the million-dollar club.

The key, my interviewees told me, is to discover for yourself the right balance of your own innate talent (everyone is good at something) and hard work. A Dallas real estate agent named JoJo said she'd noticed that relying solely on, say, an outgoing personality can be a liability. "One of my favorite sales myths is that great salespeople are always *on*," she said. "That's crazy. Can you imagine? We are already kind of obnoxious. If we were always on, we would be intolerable."

Through her career, JoJo has watched some of her peers duck the hard work and instead use their magnetism to make sales. Those agents do okay, she said, but middle-of-the-road okay; not great. Then there are those who lack the snap-crackle-pop of an extrovert but work their tails off, hour after endless hour. They do okay, too.

But *okay* has never been JoJo's goal. JoJo always knew she'd have to find the right balance of talent and work to make it big. "This is a learned aspect of being a great salesperson: The best know exactly when to turn on whatever needs to be turned on," she said. "Sometimes you click on your expertise. Sometimes you click on your ability to move quickly. Sometimes you only listen; sometimes you bust your hump getting a proposal perfect." Over time, she has learned to identify the focused effort required by each customer, for each sale.

That idea, of working hard *and* smart, is straight out of the Jordan playbook. Just like any basketball player, MJ practiced free throws over and over; he put in the hard work. But the "smart" part of his regimen was that he'd rehearse those free throws at the end of a practice, when he was exhausted, to simulate what it would be like to have to make a free throw during the crunch time at the end of a game. He didn't want to disappoint his teammates, fans, or himself by being too tired out to sink a winning free throw, so he prepared for that scenario.

LOSE NOW TO WIN LATER

I have a friend I practice tennis with every week. We do drill after drill to get us ready for matches and tournaments. One of our favorite drills is called Eleven Ball. One player hits the ball to start the play. The other player must hit the ball back. Then it's *game on*. First one to 11 wins.

My friend always wants to beat me at Eleven Ball. He will look for any opportunity to hit a winner every time. (And believe me, he can do it.) I, on the other hand, have a focused practice plan. I might decide during a game of Eleven Ball to work on my crosscourt forehand by trying to hit every shot diagonally over the net. Even though I will probably lose that game, my crosscourt forehand will get better. I use the practice to get ready for the match.

Try focused practice the next time you're about to launch a new sales pitch or strategy. Schedule a formal rehearsal or two ahead of time and role-play various client scenarios, good and bad. When it's game time, the extra effort is likely to pay off.

I'll let one of the producers in the study demonstrate how the idea of focused practice translates to sales.

It was the end of a long day, and I was at a Portland, Oregon, insurance company. I was waiting to conduct one last interview, with a casualty insurance saleswoman named Peta. Casualty insurance covers negligent acts or omissions by an organization. On a personal level, your automobile insurance is a form of casualty insurance. If you smack someone's car, you're covered.

End-of-the-day interviews are not my favorite. By then I'm usually tired, and so are the interviewees—and even superstar salespeople want to get home when their day is over. But as I waited in a conference room for Peta, I kept hearing someone talking in another conference room. This monologue, which I assumed was one very wordy side of a phone call, went on forever. Finally, I peeked around the corner and saw a woman doing a sales presentation—to no one. She was in the room by herself.

Meet Peta.

Peta told me she practices each of her presentations over and over again. She memorizes the order of the slides. She knows just when to go to a clever story to reinforce her point and when to pitch the features and benefits of her plan. She always does her run-through at the end of the business day, when she is tired. She figures if she can nail it then, she can nail it anytime.

I asked Peta if other salespeople in her office did this. She said no. "They think I'm kind of crazy," she told me. And she might be. But she is also a multimillion-dollar star seller. (By the way, despite the fact that it was the end of a long day, Peta gave me a full and lively interview.)

Which brings me to the final part of the Jordan Formula: In a winning endeavor, there is only your A game.

An NBA season consists of eighty-two matchups. And each player is expected to *bring it* at every one of them, night after night. It's what the job entails. In sales, great producers understand that every opportunity demands the best you have. Bringing your A game to every single client interaction, every single time, separates and differentiates you from the average salesperson.

I saw this for myself years before my study when I spotted Joel, a top performer at a huge pharmaceutical company, at one of his company's national sales conferences in (you guessed it) Las Vegas. Joel was one of three salespeople from the entire company asked to speak at a breakout session. The topic? These three individuals' insights into what made them successful. I was in the audience watching.

The first presenter's insights were mildly interesting. The second presenter might have been a great producer, but she had clearly prepared her speech in the elevator ride down to the conference room. Then Joel took the stage. He stepped away from the podium and commanded in a booming voice, "Stop whatever you are doing! I am going to *change your life!*"

Even then, when he was simply making a fifteen-minute presentation to a roomful of coworkers, Joel understood the energy of success better than anyone in the room. I remember straightening up in my chair. I stopped doodling idly and readied my sketchbook. I knew right away that whatever this guy was going to say, I had better be ready to capture it.

Michael Jordan didn't hold back his energy. Neither did Joel.

Remember, showing up is not enough. I recently heard a so-called expert on millennials say to a group of business leaders:

When you're looking to hire a member of this generation, you're way ahead of the game if you can just find one who will just show up.

Nope. First of all, I don't believe this expert was accurately describing millennials. Second, "just showing up" is not a strength. Whether you're a millennial or not, simply putting in an appearance will never launch you into the true moneymaking echelon of your industry. Setting low expectations does nothing for performance—yours or anybody else's. It ignores the energy it takes to excel.

Extraordinary performance is all about putting in effort and energy behind the scenes and on game day. Work at it, watch and learn, commit to bringing your best to everything you do, and you might be a superstar, too.

"EFFORTLESS" IS ANYTHING BUT

There's a story about Pablo Picasso that could be a myth. But I'm telling it anyway, because it is *that good*. Here's how it goes:

The great twentieth-century artist was sitting at a sidewalk café, when a woman approached him and exclaimed, "I am your biggest fan!" Then she asked if he would draw something on her napkin.

Picasso did as she asked, quickly producing one of those simple line drawings he was so famous for. Then he held out his doodle to the woman and said, "That will be ten thousand dollars."

"Ten thousand dollars!" she gasped. "But drawing that only took you a minute!"

Picasso's response: "No, madam, it took me a lifetime."

ESSENTIAL SECRET #3

Tell a Good Tale

I first heard Maggie's story during a workshop I was running on storytelling in business. A big financial services firm had invited seventeen of the world's most successful independent female financial advisors to a special three-day conference that included parties, sales presentations, and education. One of the components was a Creative Ventures program called the Once Upon a Time Project, which is all about how to use story as a strategic tool.

As I led these million-dollar sales pros through storytelling exercises, one participant, Maggie, seemed to already have an excellent grasp of the concept. I found out just how good she was during the break when, while making small talk, I asked her how she'd gotten her start in the business. She told me this:

Years earlier, Maggie's marriage had ended, leaving her a single mom with three kids, no career, and a future that terrified her. At church, she met an investment expert who offered to counsel her on her finances. He gave her hope by telling her about other clients who'd been in worse shape than she was and managed to carve out new lives—lives much more secure than the one she and her children seemed to be headed toward. As time went on and Maggie's financial picture brightened, she began to see herself as someone who could help others in her former situation. Not only did the friend help her straighten out her finances, he gave her hope for the future and unknowingly pointed her toward a new career.

Wow. She had just told me a great story that already had every one of the elements I had been going through in my class. I asked Maggie how many times she had shared her story, as she had it honed to perfection.

She said, "I tell it to every client."

STORY BASICS, PART 1

Every compelling story, whether a screenplay or a sales pitch, follows a similar structure. When you're crafting your own stories, pay special attention to these elements:

The beginning. Your story needs to have a starting point that launches your idea and compels your listener to stick with you as you tell it.

The middle. This is the meat of your story. It's the stuff that happens between the starting point of your journey and the ending point, and its purpose is to move the listener toward the ending.

The end. Good stories, especially business stories, must have a clear ending, and it needs to be big. A strong ending embeds itself in the listener's memory.

Begin your story dramatically. Support your idea in the middle. End with a bang!

Maggie's client base, in fact, was women, including working mothers and single mothers, groups that could connect emotionally with the circumstances Maggie had faced herself years earlier. "I want my clients to know that my background is one of difficult times, and that I can relate to them," she went on. "Their struggles are my struggles. Their barriers are mine, and I overcame them."

Every million-dollar producer in my study had a toolbox full of equipment: product knowledge, great teams to support their sales efforts, emotional connections, relationship development, and so on. All of these are important in sales. But perhaps the most creative tool these hotshots possessed, and everyone had it, was the ability to tell a compelling story. **Essential Secret #3 recognizes the crucial role storytelling plays in sales success.**

Yes, I know. Pretty much every sales book talks about the power of story. But I'm here to tell you this skill is absolutely *key* if you hope to be a million-dollar producer.

MONDAY MORNING STORYTIME

I work with a large insurance company that's based in Atlanta, with thirty-five other offices scattered around the country. When I was helping them learn how to use story to their advantage, I suggested they implement what I call a What's Going On? meeting. Now, every Monday, at every one of these locations, the sales staff gathers for thirty minutes to touch base. One of the agenda items at What's Going On? is to collect stories. The sales managers ask, "Does anyone have a great story from last week?"

After the meeting the sales managers from the various offices send their culled stories to national headquarters. The corporate marketing office gives them a quick review, selects no more than three, and crafts them into short, powerful stories shared over the company's intranet. Any broker in any office can hit the "story" button and access a fresh yarn they can use to win over a potential client.

STORY BASICS, PART 2

Steven Spielberg's films have made billions of dollars, and his collection of awards could probably fill a warehouse, because he is perhaps the most gifted storyteller of our time. Spielberg understands that good stories always have certain crucial elements. Your sales story may not be a blockbuster, but you should pay attention to:

Character. Audiences connect with the memorable heroes who drive Spielberg's stories, like the befuddled UFO-obsessed electrical lineman in *Close Encounters of the Third Kind* and the self-sacrificing Army captain in *Saving Private Ryan*. Build your story around the characters of "you" and "your client" and you'll make a similar connection.

Conflict. This is the problem the characters must overcome in order to succeed. In *Jaws* it's *How will police chief Martin Brody save his beach town from a very persistent shark?* Craft your own story around the question *What is my client's problem?*

Resolution. At the end of every Spielberg movie, the problem is solved. No hero is better at overcoming seemingly insurmountable obstacles than one Dr. Indiana Jones of *Raiders of the Lost Ark*, who managed to sneak a powerful religious artifact out of Nazi clutches and avoid being burned to a crisp. Your product or service will save your client's day: That's the theme of your sales story.

Recognizing the power of story in sales isn't just about how *you* tell *your* story. It can also be about how you get your customers to tell you theirs. Jenny and Mark, who run a Seattle advertising agency and manage huge, million-dollar accounts, know this well. Telling tales is their primary job: Every television commercial, every ad, every billboard, and every interaction they create is a story. But that's only one way they take advantage of their story-crafting talents. Jenny and Mark originate their ideas by using story development techniques to help them figure out what their clients want to say.

"We want to know what makes our clients tick," they told me. "We want to know what's important to them. We want them to tell us the story of their vision, their values, how *their* clients help shape their goals. We want to know what compels them to do what they do. We encourage the client to tell us a captivating story so we can craft that into the message we eventually create for them." Jenny and Mark are looking to form a connection between their client's product and the consumers who will hopefully buy it, and that all starts with figuring out the client's story.

How do they do that? By asking their clients a lot of deep questions. During my interview with Jenny and Mark, these two big-time producers walked me through their client engagement process. For example, one of their accounts was a high-end modern-furniture store. Every piece of furniture was sleek and stylish and very expensive. I loved the look and feel of this stuff. But even when they were wooing this furniture retailer, Jenny and Mark didn't really ask much about the furniture. Instead, they asked about the retailer's culture, vision, and dreams, questions like "What are you searching for?" If this kind of questioning doesn't come naturally to you, you might try thinking up some "Tell me" queries for your clients. (For more on "Tell me," see the introduction to this book.)

MISSION CRITICAL

The 1969 moon walk almost didn't happen. In fact, the entire moon mission may owe itself to the power of story.

On January 27, 1967, while the program was still in the testing phase, the unthinkable happened. During a routine test, the command module caught fire. In a matter of seconds it was over. Virgil "Gus" Grissom, Edward White, and Roger Chaffee perished in the fire, the first astronauts to lose their lives in pursuit of President John F. Kennedy's dream.

The incident stunned the nation, and it seemed inevitable that the entire mission would be deemed unnecessarily dangerous and that NASA would be shut down. Then, at the congressional hearings into the accident—which centered on looking for which astronaut to blame—Colonel Frank Borman was called to testify as an expert. Borman was an astronaut himself; he had been the commander of the *Apollo 8* space mission, the first manned space flight to orbit the moon.

While Borman was under questioning, one of the members of the congressional panel asked if Borman could talk a little bit about the men who'd lost their lives.

Borman proceeded to tell stories about the lost astronauts. He made their sacrifice personal. Through his stories, he helped the panel understand what it meant to be an astronaut and how these men had been real people who were missed. Borman wove a story about his lost colleagues that explained the sense of honor, duty, and country that forms the foundation of an astronaut.

It is believed that these stories, told spontaneously, saved not only the Apollo program but NASA itself.

Human beings have been telling stories since day one. Stories help us connect emotionally to ideas. In sales, a story magnifies an idea's impact. It can help a buyer connect to the outcome of his or her purchase. A story can present a solution and cement a relationship. For all these reasons and more, the most successful sales professionals constantly use story as a tool, even when they don't realize they're doing it.

Marco sells insurance as a financial investment. He is *very* good at spotting opportunities to help his clients fill gaps in their estate planning and financial portfolios. He only wants the best for his clients, and he is as likely to say a particular investment isn't right for a client's needs as he is to recommend one. Marco's unique style has earned him a loyal client base and generates referrals that keep his pipeline full. In his Los Angeles office, he has built a team that supports his goals. They, too, have benefited from Marco's style and are fiercely loyal.

As I interviewed Marco, he repeatedly credited his team members for much of his success. He said, "I would not even be eligible for this interview without them." Then he told me a story about how Abbie, a member of his administrative staff, had once rushed to Los Angeles International Airport to deliver an investment proposal to a couple of prospective clients who were headed to Paris. The couple had told her they'd hoped to have the plan to review during their flight, and Abbie decided to make that happen.

Have you ever had to drive to LAX, find parking there, and then locate a couple of people in that massive airport crowd? Well, Abbie managed to do all of those things, and now these two investors are Marco's clients. The best part of the story is that Marco had no idea any of this had happened until a month later, when the couple came in to purchase the plan and told him of Abbie's efforts.

Now, that's a pretty impressive tale, and Marco tells it whenever he wants to illustrate just how far he and his team will go to keep a client happy. It's one thing to say to a prospect, "We go the extra mile." It's far more effective to bring that idea to life through a great story. "When a client wants to know 'Why should I choose you and your team as my agent?'" Marco told me, "I say, 'Because of Abbie.'"

Paul J. Zak, PhD, the founding director of the Center for Neuroeconomics Studies at Claremont Graduate University in Claremont, California, says story has a biological effect on humans, triggering the release of oxytocin, a hormone associated with trust. If he is right, that means that when you use storytelling as a tool, you can drum up in your customers an emotion they need to feel in order to buy from you.

The story process has three parts that happen in this order:

1. DISCOVER: Choose a story to tell. During this phase you pick the right tale to fit your goal, and that begins with having an inventory of stories at the ready. When I asked Marco how many "go the extra mile" stories he had in his inventory, he smiled and said, "Many. And I keep adding to the list."

If you haven't started your own story collection, now is a good time to do that. It shouldn't be too hard: Great sales professionals' lives are full of stories of soaring success and of dismal failure. Start tracking and recording your stories in a simple notebook. This inventory of stories will lead you to the discovery process, which is about narrowing down which story in your inventory will create the impact you're looking for.

2. CRAFT: Develop the story. Notice that I use the word "craft," not the word "write." We write all day long: e-mails, text messages, notes. But we do not do much crafting.

You cannot schlock together bits and pieces of information and expect the resulting story to help you meet your sales goals. Your story should have a narrative arc—that is, a beginning that sets up a conflict, a middle in which the conflict is played out, and an end in which the conflict is resolved (ideally to the benefit of the client). The short version of Marco's Abbie story is: Beginning: A potential client made an unexpected and urgent request.

Middle: Abbie went to heroic lengths to satisfy that request. End: The client lived happily ever after.

3. TELL: Share your story with listeners. Storytelling is an art form that requires a great deal of practice. You can't just wing it. Instead, hone your performance by rehearsing it alone and in front of your team until you are so comfortable with it that you no longer feel like you're reciting lines. You don't need to repeat it word for word—in fact, if you do, you'll likely sound awkward—but you do need to know your story very well. Your telling needs to have your personality and your own style.

Superstar producers use story in *every* sales encounter. If you want to get the highest possible numbers and achieve your career goals, start by making story the most important tool in your own sales toolbox.

THE SIX-WORD CHALLENGE

Legend has it that the great writer Ernest Hemingway once bet a group of friends $10 that he could write an entire story in six words. When his friends took him up on it, he wrote the following:

For sale: Baby shoes, never worn.

He collected $10 from everyone at the table.

At Creative Ventures, we use this technique to help salespeople get to the very essence of what they're trying to say. If you have to get your message across in only six words, you're forced to create a very SIMPLE narrative. For example, Maggie, the financial advisor, used these six words to explain that, at the most basic level, she is selling peace of mind:

"You will sleep on windy nights."

Meaning, "When things get rough, you can relax."

Try this exercise to hone your story skills and create the building blocks of any number of narratives.

ESSENTIAL SECRET #4

Make Friends First

I'm about to tell you something that will seem crazy. Here goes: **Make your client a friend before you make him or her a customer. Forming a relationship with a client is more important than making a sale—at least in the beginning.** When I share this particular secret with people, a lot of them say things like, "Are you out of your mind?"

I get it. *Don't even mention whatever it is you are selling until you've built a solid relationship with your client* is a counterintuitive idea. Salespeople love the stuff their companies make and/or do. When you love your product or service, you want to hit potential clients with a full-on shock-and-awe bombardment of data, comparative analysis, statistically significant facts, and so on. You want your hoped-for client to know that what you are selling sits at the pinnacle of the market.

Forget that nagging desire. Shift your strategy and ditch the sales pitch, just temporarily. The first time you meet a new potential client, focus all of your attention on the relationship you're creating with this new customer. In sales—at least if you want to be in the big leagues—this relationship is so critical that the product or service you're selling is almost secondary.

This concept is so important that I am going to repeat it, just to be sure you have absorbed it: Essential Secret #4 recognizes that million-dollar producers are not in the sales business. They are in the relationship business. Yes, they sell stuff. But they have risen to the million-dollar level because they understand that they're playing the long game. They know that by taking time to form a strong and lasting relationship, they won't just score one sale; they'll score many sales over many years with the same client. They have risen well above their competition and achieved their success because they focus tremendous attention on these relationships.

Now back to Make Friends First.

When sales teams hear this particular secret, it's like I've tossed a wrench into a set of gears. The conversation grinds to a stop. People don't believe me. It is counterintuitive—it goes against the accepted way of doing business. Perhaps it even goes against common sense.

In this case, that's good.

THE POWER OF COUNTERINTUITIVE THINKING

One of my favorite stories of successful outside-the-box thinking stars Abraham Wald, a mathematical genius born in Austria-Hungary in 1902. Wald escaped the pre–World War II Nazi regime, came to New York, and ended up working for the U.S. war effort in what was called the Statistical Research Group.

The group was made up of thinkers who used math to find solutions to various military problems, including this one: *How do we keep our bomber aircraft from getting shot down?*

The obvious answer was *Add more armor*. But bombers, like the B-17 Flying Fortress, were big, heavy planes. These lumbering giants were instrumental to winning the war, but they were already as slow as snails in the sky, and reinforcing them would only make them bigger, heavier, and slower. The key would be to use as little extra reinforcement as possible, and only in places that really needed more protection.

The military was already on the case. When bombers that had been shot at were able to make it back to the ground, the military would check out where the bullet holes were and add armor to those areas.

Makes sense, right?

Hold on, said Wald. *You're going about this all wrong. You are adding armor to the strongest parts of the plane.*

How did he know these were the strongest parts? Well, he realized that, despite the bullet holes, planes that had been shot at in these areas had still landed in one piece. Wald suggested that these were the areas that did not need armor. Instead, he said, use the armor elsewhere on the planes. Wald had noticed that the planes that had been shot at and still landed in one piece never had bullet holes near the engines. That led him to the conclusion that the planes that never made it back were the ones that had been hit near the engines. His solution: add armor there.

And that's what the military did. Wald's counterintuitive thinking no doubt saved the lives of numerous pilots and crew. While sales isn't usually a life-or-death matter, looking at problems differently can turn you into a business genius. Wald took people who were sure of their approach and led them in a different, much better direction. The lesson: Don't immediately dismiss counterintuitive ideas.

Now I'll give you an idea of how a superstar producer goes about implementing Essential Secret #4. Enter William, better known to everyone as Billy, a sales heavyweight in a futuristic field right out of a sci-fi movie. Billy sells robotic surgery equipment. Yep, robots that the surgeons direct to cut into you (think of a scalpel crossed with a video game). Robot-assisted equipment can be used for delicate work like eye surgery, where precision is, obviously, of utmost importance, and even the tiniest shake of a surgeon's hand can be disastrous.

The machines Billy's company makes aren't cheap—they can run as much as $2 million—so, as you might imagine, Billy isn't selling one of them a day, and he isn't selling dozens to the same doctor or hospital. He's constantly courting new customers. His sales cycle is a long one, and even though these devices are pretty miraculous, during the process you won't find Billy making long speeches about their many technological wonders. In any one deal he closes, he has spent about 95 percent of that time building rapport with the buyers rather than pushing his product.

Billy is a master of the old-fashioned art of conversation. And when it comes to talking to hospital administrators, expert surgeons, chief financial officers, and wealthy donors, Billy is like a choreographer. He moves step by step through his conversational formula—ask the question, listen to the answer, share his expertise—all to get to know the decision makers and build strong, solid relationships with them.

Through all of this conversational back-and-forth, Billy is never making a formal sales pitch. In fact, he may go through many meetings and never mention the product. This market is unique, Billy knows every nuance necessary to make things happen, and he's taking a long view of the process.

We'll get back to Billy in a little bit. Right now, let's take a look at the technique Billy uses, one that dates all the way to ancient Greece. Allow me to take you back to approximately four hundred years before Christ, to the time of togas and the birth of Western philosophy.

It was around this time that one of the greatest thinkers in history, Aristotle, wrote on topics including philosophy, math—especially geometry—and biology. He also gave us rhetoric.

What is rhetoric? you might be thinking.

Rhetoric is the art of persuasion. At his school of higher learning, the Lyceum, Aristotle pondered the great questions of his day and used a process that was wonderfully SIMPLE (see Essential Secret #1) to gain the intellectual advantage and bring his students around to his way of thinking. His process, when applied properly, is the ideal way to make a sale.

Rhetoric, according to Aristotle, is made up of three parts:

ETHOS. Establish your credibility. ("Here's why you should trust me.")

PATHOS. Appeal to your listener's emotions. ("Here's why you should care about what I'm going to say.")

LOGOS. Use logic to persuade the listener. ("Here are the facts that back up my argument.")

So how does this formula fit the counterintuitive Make Friends First model? Let's modernize it and apply it to sales by renaming the three parts TRUST, EMOTION, and LOGIC. Billy wins clients with relationship-building tactics straight out of Aristotle's rulebook. How does Billy do it?

TRUST. Establish a connection. ("Let's be buddies.")

In Billy's first contact with hoped-for buyers, he has no other goal than to get to know them a little and let them get to know him. Remember, no one walks into Billy's office and says, "Can you wrap up that highly precise piece of medical equipment and put it in my car?" No one approaches him and asks, "Mind if I take that thing for a test drive?" There are going to be a lot of conversations before Billy makes a sale, and he uses the first one to start off on the right foot. Billy's success is all about the process.

Think of this first meeting as a greeting. Not the kind where you say, "Hey, how's it going?" and don't really care about the answer, but the kind in which you're genuinely interested. Billy really wants to get to know the person or people he's dealing with. He'll ask, "What's your background? Where did you go to school? How do you like working here? What's the best thing about this place?"

Now, he will likely already know a lot of this, because Billy never goes into a Let's Be Buddies meeting without finding out as much as he can beforehand about whomever he's getting together with. From LinkedIn to Google, from professional journals to trade associations, Billy will have done Sherlock Holmes–level background research. Billy behaves like a great trial lawyer cross-examining a witness, where the rule of thumb is: *Never ask a question you don't already know the answer to.* His goal is to go into a meeting armed with as much basic information as he can so the answers he gets don't catch him unawares. Remember that this getting-to-know-you meeting is really about establishing trust. To the client, it seems like a friendly and organic conversation, but the million-dollar producer has come prepared.

By the way, this meeting may not even involve the buyer. Billy often has to get past a couple of gatekeepers before he has his first conversation with the person who has the checkbook. Still, the process is pretty much the same. (For more on gatekeepers, see Secret #11, Charm the Gatekeepers.)

EMOTION. Show your clients you relate to their problem or need. ("I get it.")

If Billy is lucky enough to score a second meeting—and he probably will be—he'll use it to prove to the client that he cares about the exact same thing they do: the health and happiness of their patients. The buyer of Billy's company's robotic equipment may be a doctor or a hospital administrator, but the patients are the ones who will ultimately benefit. So Billy wants to learn everything he can about those people. (Again, he will actually already know much of this, thanks to his pre-research and his years of experience in the industry.) His strategy is to let the client—the doctor or hospital—know *I'm here to meet your needs, which in turn will help you meet your patients' needs.*

Stage two can last for a while. There could easily be multiple "I get it" meetings. Doesn't matter. This is all part of the process.

Most great relationships are built on emotion. So the "I get it" phase is a critical component of any sales process. People buy on emotion and support their purchase with logic, even when they're buying a scientific machine that costs a couple of million bucks.

Have you noticed that Billy still hasn't gone into much detail about what he's selling?

LOGIC. Connect your product to their problem. ("Here's the obvious solution to your needs.")

A product as specific as Billy's requires a lot of explanation, and Billy understands that. But stage three may be the first time he actually brings up statistics and specs. Billy calls this his "The proof is in the pudding" stage. Here he connects everything he has learned about his clients, their needs, and their patients' needs to the wonders of the machines he is selling. Here he uses storytelling to offer proof of his product's utility. He may bring up the age of the surgeons and how physically taxing it is to be on one's feet performing surgery, and then mention that with his machine surgeons can remain seated, reducing fatigue and potential errors. He might suggest that prospective clients contact other hospitals and doctors who already have the device: "I want you to hear how effective it is from actual users, not from my marketing materials."

Billy has established trust. He's learned about his client's problem and made it clear that he got it. Now he has used logic to solve the problem.

Billy's close rate is sensational, and this is not a guy selling blenders at Macy's. (I don't mean to downplay the blender; without it, Margarita Friday would not exist. I just want you to remember that Billy is selling about as specialized and expensive a machine as exists on the planet to a very limited number of very smart and choosy people.)

Billy is counterintuitive and relationship-driven. His classic Aristotelian three-part strategy focuses on creating rapport with his buyers before he gets to what he's selling.

Yes, this is a hard strategy to master. Developing relationships—selling yourself first, before you ever talk about your product or service—takes a ton of self-control.

ON THE MENU

Billy's product has a lengthy sales cycle, so he gets the benefit of playing the long game. He has time to apply his persuasive sales strategy. But even in a fast transaction you can build a relationship through the thoughtful application of trust, emotion, and logic. I recently took some clients to dinner at a very nice restaurant where the waiter followed old Aristotle's road map to a T:

When one of my clients asked, "What's good tonight?" the waiter replied that he'd sampled the specials at the daily staff meeting. He established trust. He then said the salmon was, and I quote, "heavenly." He appealed to our emotions. Lastly he said, "It's the best value on the menu." Logic.

BOOM. In just a moment, he had built a micro-relationship with all of us, and guess what? *Three salmon orders, please.*

He was right: The salmon *was* delicious.

Here is how to adapt Billy's three-part process to your own persuasive strategy:

○ *TRUST* starts with building a relationship.

When you're getting to know a client, it helps to do a little background research on him or her to discover key bits of information that will help you connect. One way to organize this information is to divide a sheet of paper in half and label one side "Personal" and the other "Professional." As you look into your potential new client, take notes on things you uncover that fit either in the personal column (hobbies, interests, family) or the professional column (designations, product use history, past product relationships). This exercise will provide you with the talking points for your first meeting. Using these conversation starters will help your client open up more quickly, and you will soon find yourself having a real conversation, making a human connection. You're on your way to building trust.

> ○ *EMOTION* is about showing your clients you're on their side.

It's time to think like your customer. Approach your second meeting like a listening session. All you're going to do here is focus on what your client's problems are. Again, resist the temptation to solve those problems right now by jumping into a sales pitch for your product. The goal here is simply to build on the personal connection you worked so hard to win in the first meeting. A premature pitch could endanger your relationship, because it will make your client think you don't actually care that much—that you're really just out to make a quick buck.

So, instead of a pitch, ask your client to explain the issues in play. Try a couple of open-ended "Tell me" questions: "Tell me how your problem is impacting your business." "Tell me about your market." Then practice active listening (a technique we will explore in Secret #8, W.A.I.T.).

○ *LOGIC* is about meeting your client's needs.

The goal here is to get your client to conclude that your product or service will solve his or her problem. It's not an easy bridge to build, but you have already taken two steps of this three-step process. You have gotten to know the client on a personal and professional level. You have spent time in a problem-defining phase where you invited the client to explain his or her needs.

You've got the trust. You know what the problem is. Now make your product or service the answer.

What if you do happen to sell blenders? The TRUST-EMOTION-LOGIC model doesn't fit every sales situation. It's really best for the kind of major purchases that require a customer to take a big leap of faith and write a big check. Plenty of salespeople, particularly those just starting out, are in the low-risk, single-transaction business. Customers don't go to Best Buy or a department store *thinking* of buying a blender; they go to buy a blender. In the coming weeks, months, or years, they are not likely to follow up their blender purchase with additional kitchen gadgets sold by the same salesperson. Thus, the transaction doesn't require the same level of deep relationship building.

However, even if you find yourself in the blender department, Billy's approach gives you an inside look at a career-building skill.

And if, like Billy, you are selling complicated products or long-term services, Aristotle's persuasive technique has stood the test of time. If you use it, you will develop a genuine friendship with your client in which the sale is simply the silver lining.

— *Part II* —

Client Relationship Secrets

Treat Your Customers the Way Million-Dollar Producers Treat Theirs

SECRET #5

One Level Above

There's a reason Gordon is a gazillionaire. Gordon—remember him? The guy who couldn't go for fifteen minutes without checking his phone?—sells a particular fund at a leading financial services firm with offices in the U.S. and worldwide. Gordon keeps his company's highest-profile, deepest-pocketed clients happy by exceeding their expectations a little bit more every year.

Gordon understands two truths about his business: First, he has no control over the product he sells. Second, similar investment products are readily available from his competitors. Gordon knows the thing that sets him apart is the way he treats his clients. So every twelve months, as he sets his goals for the coming year, Gordon plans one new way to improve the client experience.

The client experience is the combination of customer service, assistance, and perks that you, the sales professional, bring to your customers. It's separate from the product or service you sell. In sales, a lot of factors are out of your hands, including your competitors' actions, the economy, and the political climate. The client experience is one thing that is always in your control.

For example, a couple of years ago Gordon got the idea to

provide each of the company's elite clients with a special blue-and-gold metal card. It looks like a credit card and is emblazoned with the client's name and a private phone number.

If you're one of Gordon's twenty-five or thirty top customers, you can call this number any time of day or night. An operator will answer within two rings and immediately track down and connect you to the person at the company you wish to speak to. It's a thoughtful perk that separates Gordon and the company he works for from all the others.

Even better—especially for Gordon, who is already on the phone most of the day—it was one simple improvement in the client experience that was relatively easy to implement.

This strategy, which I call One Level Above, or OLA, is all about the power of the single-step ascent. Here is the concept behind Secret #5: **Take one part of the client experience one level above where it is now.** It's not about what you should be doing differently. It is about what you can do better.

The most appealing aspect about OLA is that it's finite. It's manageable. You can continue to spend most of your energy on doing your actual job because you only have to tackle improving one aspect of the client experience, one step at a time.

Think about it. Great salespeople often find themselves trapped in endless meetings and on mind-numbing conference calls, and buried under avalanches of e-mail, most of which takes them away from their primary task: to sell. The OLA strategy is just the opposite. It focuses on one critical action. That action is specifically designed to *increase* your sales by escalating the elements that make you and your customer service unique.

WHEN LESS IS MORE

Salespeople love the idea of *more*. I go to the movies and ask for a medium Dr Pepper, and the person at the concession counter will try to sell me the jumbo size for an extra quarter. No, thanks, I tell him; I only want a medium. He says, "It's only another twenty-five cents, dude!"

Yes, I realize the jumbo size is more economical. I just don't want a hot tub full of Dr Pepper.

Don't automatically assume OLA means "more."

Ready to put OLA into action? It only takes three steps:

1. Establish your starting point. All mountain ascents begin at a base camp. It's here that climbers make sure they have the right equipment and assess conditions before scaling the peak in front of them.

In OLA, you find your starting point by truly understanding your client's current experience with you. To do that, you need to put yourself in your client's shoes. This can be the hardest and most difficult part of the entire strategy.

To start, take some quiet time and write down your understanding of the client experience. Think about how you approach a new prospect, how you follow up after that first contact, and how you check in once you've made the sale. At each step, how do you treat your customer? Are there meetings, dinners, and events? Are there reports? What does all of that look like? What does the experience look like for your longtime clients? Do they receive the same level of care as your new clients?

Next, round up your team and put them through the same exercise. Get input. If you are gutsy enough, grab a few clients and treat them to a meal at which the agenda is having them talk about their client experience. You'll be surprised at how open customers can be, especially if they know the meeting isn't a product pitch. (To learn how superstar producers get their clients to open up, see Secret #6, Build Your "Like" Platform.)

Now that you have done all of your research, consolidate this information so you have a full, honest picture of what it's like to do business with you.

2. Create a master list of OLA ideas. Now it's time to dream up any and every action you can think of that might improve any part of the client experience one level above where it is now. (Some designers and creative types refer to the process of brainstorming as "ideation.") Consider what you have learned about the client experience and dream up some possible actions that, when applied in an effective way, could make it better. Write down every idea you generate. At this point in the process, no idea is a bad idea. Well, some of them will be bad, but write them down anyway.

Next, narrow down your ideas to one. (Why only one? See Essential Secret #1, SIMPLE.) One single, substantial action item that will elevate one aspect of the client experience one level above where it is now.

To get down to a single idea, you'll need to simultaneously put yourself in your own shoes and in your customers' shoes. You have to think not just *Will this make our clients happier?* and *Will it help us stand out?* but *Can we do it? Is it financially feasible?* and *Are we equipped to make it happen?*

Narrowing down all of your ideas to just one is really tough. You can get emotionally attached to an idea and have a hard time letting go of it, even when it doesn't serve your goals. A detached observer, whether an outside consultant or just a smart person from a different division of your company, can help you get perspective. And remember, you can always go back and reconsider the discarded ideas for next year's OLA. Another tip: It's often easier to reduce your ideas a few at a time. If you have ten strong ideas, reduce that list to five. From five, go to three, and from three to that one idea that will create impact.

3. Put your idea into action. I cannot tell you how many OLA strategies I have been involved with that began with a big bang but ran out of momentum as time went on. How do you bring this new piece of the client experience to life and keep it on track? By making one person responsible for driving it.

At Creative Ventures, we call this individual the "Accountable." The Accountable builds a team to help put the OLA into action but is still the single person who's ultimately in charge. Since the Accountable bears the responsibility for making the OLA happen, it's important that he or she be really invested in it. The Accountable should come from the team that dreamed it up in the first place. He or she must truly want to take ownership of the OLA.

Almost all of the OLA strategies I have been involved with were accomplished with a single person in charge. One idea. One person. One level above.

Stavros, like Gordon, is another OLA expert. Stavros is the sales leader at a large regional office for a global insurance company. Every fall he starts planning for the upcoming sales year, and his planning always begins with thinking of a new OLA. Stavros's OLA always goes beyond any requirements the company sets for its salespeople overall.

One of Stavros's favorite areas to improve is points of contact. "Points of contact" means "every possible way a client might be able to get in touch with you and your team." The concept of points of contact is deeply important in sales, as it is the genesis of business as well as, often, the first impression a new client has of a salesperson. So Stavros spends a lot of time figuring out how to improve in this area.

One point of contact is, of course, the phone. Since Stavros's busy regional office gets a high volume of calls, one year he and his team decided to focus specifically on improving his clients' phone experience. Stavros wanted to know: What was his clients' experience with the phone? How often did incoming calls go to voice mail? How often did clients get to interact with a live person?

After learning the answers to these questions, Stavros and his team settled on an OLA. They called it Three Rings. It meant that no caller would have to hear more than three rings before a real, live human being answered the phone.

Every person on Stavros's six-person team committed to answering the phone. Not just the account managers or receptionists, but everyone. If you didn't know the answer to the caller's question, or if the caller was looking for someone other than you, you took a message the old-fashioned way: by writing it down and walking it over to the person it was meant for. If you wanted to forward the caller to a coworker's voice mail, you would do so only after asking the caller's permission.

It took almost two months for the three-ring protocol to become the norm. It wasn't easy, but it was the only OLA on the table. And it has made a huge difference in the client experience. In fact, clients consistently bring it up as one of the things they like best about doing business with Stavros and his team. An OLA must become part of your company DNA before you can move on to the next OLA. Its application has to be consistent and continuous. This is hard to do, which is why there is always only one OLA in play at any given time.

The real point of OLA is to move away from a strategy of adding more and more to-dos that end up being poorly executed or forgotten, and instead focus on a single critical action that can make a substantive difference in your clients' experience.

Oh, and what do you do at the end of a year, after you've achieved your OLA? You move on to a new OLA. (Remember those ideas you put aside in Step 2?)

I call this the Horizon Model. You have probably noticed that when you keep moving toward the horizon, you never get there. With OLA, that is a good thing. Your continuing quest to improve the client experience never—and I mean *never*—reaches completion.

Ironically, sometimes the Horizon Model includes getting rid of past OLAs. Peter and Juan, two salesmen turned management executives at one of America's largest financial companies, regularly jettison previous years' OLAs as part of their annual OLA planning process.

Which might make you wonder: Why would these guys take away from their clients something that successfully improved the client experience?

Here's the deal: If you choose one new OLA to implement every year, over time the OLAs accumulate. If you have too many to attend to, eventually they become counterproductive, eating away at valuable time and energy. So each year Peter and Juan list every OLA program still in play at their huge company and rank the OLAs in order of perceived value, based on any shifts that have occurred in market conditions or client preferences. They note how many clients take advantage of the OLA and whether that number has increased or decreased over time. By the time Peter and Juan have gotten toward the bottom of the list, they have identified at least a couple of OLA programs that are no longer worth their staff's time and effort.

One recently removed OLA was a career-coaching service the two had set up for their clients. When they originally started the program it was popular and successful, but after a number of years it had lost its luster. Only a handful of clients were still taking advantage of the service. It was time to phase that one out.

Sometimes there are even OLAs on the list that Peter and Juan had completely forgotten about. If you can't remember an OLA, that's also a good sign that it's no longer critical to a unique and dynamic client experience, and you can let it go. By culling the old, you can make way for a new improvement that will keep your clients in a constant state of amazement and help *you* reach the million-dollar level.

IF IT QUACKS LIKE A DUCK...

"We don't do *sales*. We do *client acquisition*," the people at the architectural firm told me. Ah, okay. If that's what you want to call it.

This firm was a consulting client of mine, a big-time company that was not involved in my 21 Secrets study. While they didn't consider themselves to be in sales, they'd asked me to help them figure out how to hold on to existing clients and attract new business.

I thought they could benefit from the OLA strategy. So even though they "weren't in sales," I suggested it to them, too. Soon every division in this large firm, which specializes in megaprojects like schools and stadiums, was off on its own OLA hunt, each looking for one thing it could do to boost the company's overall profile in this incredibly competitive market.

The OLA the company eventually implemented was something called the Client Book. These days, after a project is completed, the firm gives each client a bound book of color photographs that tells the story of the project, from groundbreaking to ribbon cutting. Aside from being a fantastic souvenir and record, the book is a powerful visual reminder that keeps the firm at the top of the client's mind long after the project is finished. The book differentiates this company in a very visible way.

Take from this story two lessons: One, whether you call it "client acquisition" or something else, if you are in business, you are in the sales business. *Every* business has to sell itself. Second, OLA isn't just for sales departments. It's a strategy that can work anywhere.

SECRET #6

Build Your "Like" Platform

I had just finished up a speech to a roomful of financial advisors in Orlando and was leaving to interview another one of my sales superstars. I stepped out of the convention center and got hit by that famous Florida heat and humidity. It felt like I was inhaling the Gulf of Mexico. After the briefest moment I was already in a deep sweat.

About a thirty-minute drive later I arrived at a large Porsche dealership, where, unlike me, not one car on the lot revealed any weather-related wear and tear. Even sitting there out in the elements, each one looked fresh off the factory floor.

Inside, the showroom was air-conditioned and immaculate. It looked like the bridge of the Starship *Enterprise* and was filled with cars that resembled sculptures. This particular dealership can only be described as a Porsche superstore, and every vehicle was a fantasy car.

A salesman came up to me. "Beautiful, aren't they?"

"Yes, they are," I replied.

"You know one of the best things?" he continued. "The smell."

I hadn't focused on this, but he was right: The entire room

81

smelled like a new car. Still, at this point in my study of top producers, I was noticing pretty much everything about any encounter I had with a salesperson, and what I had noticed just now was that there had been no "May I help you?" or "Anything I can show you?" from this guy. Instead, just a couple of friendly observations.

"You must be Steve," the salesman said when I told him I was looking for Jeff. Jeff had mentioned I would be stopping by, the guy continued, escorting me to a conference room while explaining, "He's just finishing up a 'like' meeting."

A "like" meeting. I hadn't heard it phrased that way before, but I did recognize the concept from other interviews. *Hmm,* I thought. *Might be a pattern.* Turned out it was.

Inside the conference room, Jeff and three colleagues on his sales team were wrapping up their meeting. On a whiteboard was a series of statements:

- So much knowledge
- Freedom from pressure
- Beeline from purchase to service
- Follow-up after purchase
- Soft touch

I realized pretty quickly, as you probably have, too, that these were all things the dealership's customers had said they liked about the sales experience.

The meeting adjourned, and I followed Jeff to his office. (Unlike many dealerships whose salespeople work out of open cubicles, here in Porscheland they had private, well-appointed spaces.)

When I meet an interviewee for the first time, I usually give my opening spiel about the purpose of the study, the "Tell me" questions, and so on. This time, I launched right in and asked about the scene we had just left. Looking at that whiteboard, I'd had a realization that could not have been more obvious:

People like to do business with people they like.

Duh, right? But as basic as it is, this little truth is also absolutely critical to sales success. There are two reasons why.

First, consider the opposite statement: People will go out of their way not to do business with people they don't like. If you receive bad service at a restaurant, you will go out of your way not to return. If someone suggests that restaurant in the future, you'll probably say, "I'm never going there again. I hate that place."

Second, consider this: Most salespeople, including your competition, spend little to no time figuring out what their customers actually enjoy about them.

So if there's one way you want your customers to feel about you, the word that should come to mind is "like."

(This might go against conventional sales wisdom. I have heard more than one person say that being trustworthy is more important than being likable. *Huh?* Have you ever heard a customer say, "Oh, Steve. I trust him, but I don't like him at all"? Never. "Like" leads to "trust." It's not the other way around.)

THE DUH FACTOR

Most people brush off obvious-sounding advice. We assume if "everybody knows that," it won't have much impact. Yet, when we realize how important these obvious truths are, we slap ourselves upside the head and wonder, *Why didn't I think of that?*

I call this the Duh Factor.

It took humankind five thousand years to add wheels to luggage, and now you wouldn't think about bringing a wheelless bag to the airport. It also was a pretty recent decision to change the ketchup bottle to an upside-down design, so that we no longer have to slap it on the bottom like a newborn to get the ketchup out. DUH! Both of these inspirations prove that genius is really just the application of the obvious.

Some of the advice in this book, too, is pretty obvious. But here's the difference between million-dollar producers and everyone else: Everyone knows it's important that customers like their salesperson. The superstars don't just *know* it; they *work* at it.

But back to Jeff. Jeff is the leading salesman at his Porsche dealership, which is one of the world's largest and most successful. The "like" meeting was, in fact, a regular event among all the members of the dealership's sales force, who gather in small groups to go over exactly what their clients enjoy about buying expensive cars from them. Some of the information is culled from client surveys. Some comes from the salespeople themselves. (They're all required to keep sales journals and record observations about each client interaction.) The "like" meetings have a purpose: The dealership wants to be able to replicate the behaviors and actions that make their customers happy.

As for Jeff, his status as this dealership's top salesman has to do with his super-laser focus on "like." In an organization in which "like" is already important, Jeff studies each sales survey, makes meticulous notes in his journal, and listens intently as his colleagues discuss their client successes and their missed opportunities.

"Like" is all about emotions. There's nothing rational about it. In fact, oftentimes people don't know why they like something. Why do you like pineapple upside-down cake? Why do you like the song "Desperado"? Who knows. You just do.

In sales, "like" is about your clients' feelings. Specifically, it's about how *you* make *them* feel. Do they leave happy after doing business with you? Do they feel they're in good hands? Do they think you're nice? If you are the orchestrator of these feelings, you are a maestro of "like."

That's critical to building your book of business, because "like" taps into the emotional connection customers make between the product or service they just purchased and the person—you— who made that purchase happen. As we've already discussed, customers usually buy on emotion and later justify that buying decision with a backfill of logic, reason, and judgment. (This jus- tification usually works, too, except maybe when you're buying your fourteenth pair of red shoes if you're a shoe person or, if you golf, whatever new gizmo you think is sure to finally make you hit that little ball straight.)

Here is the real power of "like": Even when things are not equal—when, for example, your competitor's product or service has slightly better pricing or features—a customer will return to the salesperson he likes. Your customer is searching for a mutually beneficial and rewarding purchasing experience. He gets this when he likes you.

Just think about it: What better sales strategy can there be than to discover what your clients like about you and . . . do more of that?

Let's take a closer look at the items on the whiteboard at Jeff's meeting. How did Jeff fit into the comments from satisfied customers?

- "So much knowledge." All clients like a smart sales professional, but in Jeff's world, expertise is extra important. Porsche drivers are passionate about their cars and could not imagine doing business with someone who doesn't share that love. Jeff's love for Porsches is obvious. He can recite every statistic about any model, from its horsepower to the stitching on its seats. He is just as knowledgeable about older models that aren't on the sales floor anymore, which is important: Many of his buyers are trading in their old Porsches for new ones.
- "Freedom from pressure." Buyers hate pushy salespeople. Jeff is a little lucky here, because his dealership expressly

forbids its sales force from pressuring customers. In fact, they're trained to not even approach a potential buyer right away. When they do make contact, as I learned firsthand, they keep the conversation light.

○ "Beeline from purchase to service." Luxury-car buyers may develop a relationship with their sales professional, but over the years they'll *really* bond with their service guy. That's fine with Jeff. Many of his customers are repeat buyers because of this key strategy: Immediately after making a sale, Jeff escorts the new owner to his dealership's service department and introduces the client to his or her own personal service person. It's a nice touch customers love. It's also crucial to Jeff's future sales to that customer. After you buy a car, you don't see your sales guy. The relationship you develop is with your service guy. Jeff wants to make sure that relationship is a satisfying one for the customer, because it helps ensure that in a few years, when it's time for a new car, the customer will stay with Jeff's dealership.

○ "Follow-up after the purchase." Luxury buyers have relationships with their products, and if you're the person who sold them their ride, they'll extend that relationship to you if you artfully and elegantly stay in contact. One of Jeff's signature gestures is that he takes a photo of every client with his or her new car and sends it to them in a little frame with the dealership logo on it. Nice touch. Later, every time a Porsche wins an auto race, he'll send his customers a photograph of the winning car, with the client Photoshopped into the picture as if he or she were the driver.

○ "Soft touch." This is the all-important client contact that isn't related to the product. Jeff sends his customers hand-written thank-you notes, birthday cards, and holiday gifts. He also knows a lot about his customers. *A lot.* One of his longtime customers is a University of Florida alumnus and a huge Gators fan. Jeff, who's also an alum, regularly pulls sports news from his University of Florida Google feed and sends it to the guy.

BE WELL LIKED

What are some of the key qualities that make customers like you? During our study, some of the same descriptions kept coming up:

Friendly. One of the managers at the UPS Store in my little Texas community is possibly the most standoffish person I have ever come in contact with. This guy never smiles, makes eye contact, or engages in conversation. Compared to all the other really friendly folks who work there, he sticks out like an elephant at a hamster party. I go out of my way to avoid him.

Attentive. Jeff knew his customer was a Gators fan from paying attention to him. You, too, should listen and remember when your clients tell you things. (Here's a good use of people's business cards: When someone hands you one, jot down a simple fact about them on the back.)

Empathetic. How sensitive are you? Can you look at your product or service from your client's point of view? Jeff totally relates to his customers' fantasies of driving around in a Porsche, and it shows in his pitch.

Real. Are you fair, honest, and genuine? At the outdoorsy retailer

L.L.Bean, where Joan from Essential Secret #1 took me to buy some replacement gear, it is not unheard-of for a salesperson to say, "We don't carry the kind of shoe you're looking for, but you might be able to find it at . . ." and then recommend a competitor, if that's what it takes to help a customer. *That* is being real. (For more on being genuine, see Secret #20, You Can't Fake Real.)

With Jeff, I showed you what an internal "like" meeting is all about. Now let's take a look at an external "like" meeting.

Kathleen—"Kat" to all her friends (and it seems *everyone* is her friend)—is in the pharmaceutical business, selling cardiology drugs, a category that's booming. Kat lives in Indianapolis and has some of the best client relationships I've ever heard of. Her clients treat her as well as she treats them.

She could easily get a call from a customer who asks her to lunch and picks up the tab, even after Kat explains that she could put the bill on her own expense account. Her clients actually send *her* birthday cards. Kat also plays on a client's bowling team. Basically, her customers just really dig her.

Think that's random luck? Guess again. It is the result of Kat's "like" strategy.

Kat gathers lots of data about what makes her clients happy. She'll sometimes send them brief online surveys she creates herself, with questions such as "Did you feel cared for?" Even more remarkable, her clients also tell her these things in person, at what she calls her "From the Horse's Mouth" gatherings.

Kat's events are a little different from the usual client get-togethers you find in sales. Hers are small and informal. They always include a meal and some kind of fun demonstration. They never last more than an hour. (Food, fun, and a very short time commitment are all crucial to this formula.) No sales pitch, no product positioning, and no budget questions. There's only one topic on the agenda. Kat wants to know from her clients: "What do you like about the way I conduct business?"

One of these gatherings was a breakfast meeting featuring gourmet donuts from a popular local bakery. Kat invited the donut maker to come and talk briefly about the creative process that brought each flavor into existence. There were maple-bacon donuts, Cap'n Crunch donuts, and even hash brown donuts. The donut part lasted fifteen minutes, and after that it was on to the matter at hand.

At her meetings Kat asks questions that start with "How do you like . . . ?" and are structured around the various parts of her sales process. She might focus on the frequency of her calls or the complexity of her pitch. She invites different clients to each gathering and records all of their comments. One result of these informational meetings is that she has changed the way she introduces new products. Her clients liked her presentation style, they told her, but sometimes found the content overwhelming.

So she has made her pitch SIMPLE.

The idea is: Your clients will gladly tell you what you need to know if you just ask. And if you ask in a creative and fun manner, they will tell you over and over again.

*   *   *

You may have noticed that I haven't really gone into the flip side of "like": "dislike." Here is an interesting aspect of Kat's gatherings: She doesn't really have to ask any awkward "What *don't* you like about doing business with me?" questions. When you pose a "like" question, you will naturally get some criticism. For instance, ask, "What do you like about my presentation style?" and at some point somebody might tell you, "I don't like all the stuff you give us to read."

Want to turn that into a "like"? Before your next presentation, take all of that reading and boil it down. Tell your client, "All of the details and backup are available if you want it, but if you don't, here is a one-page summary." BANG—you just turned a "dislike" into a "like" without ever having to ask a negative question.

Surveys, sales journals, meetings—building your "like" platform seems like a lot of work. But if you really think about it, making use of this basic truth—**people like to do business with people they like**—might get you into the million-dollar club. Wouldn't you like that?

SECRET #7

They'll Know It When They See It

In 1964, the United States Supreme Court heard a case centered on an unusual question: What is pornography?

An Ohio court had fined a theater owner for showing an "obscene" movie—a French art film called *The Lovers*. The theater owner appealed, and the case ultimately landed at the highest court. After the Supreme Court justices watched the racy movie, Justice Potter Stewart issued the now-famous definition of hardcore pornography: "I know it when I see it." (Stewart went on to deem the film *not* pornographic, and the theater owner won the appeal.)

THE ELEPHANT TEST

In business, law, and other professions, the concept "It's hard to describe, but you'll know it when you see it" is also sometimes called the elephant test. The term probably comes from an old parable about a group of men in a dark room who are trying to explain what an elephant is just by touching specific parts. One guy touches the tail and describes the elephant as a rope; another touches the animal's side and says the elephant is a wall; and so on. Because no one can see the whole thing, each man's understanding of the elephant is limited and, ultimately, incorrect.

Sometimes it's easier to *show* your clients what you mean than it is to try to explain it to them. Especially when you're selling something that isn't concrete, like an idea or a service as opposed to a car or a house. In these cases, visuals such as props and photos help your clients quickly understand your point.

In the spirit of "showing," I'm going to let three of my interviewees demonstrate what I mean.

Let's begin with Ryan, a master showman who treats each sales presentation like a stage performance. Ryan manages a team of investment wholesalers, the middlemen who help financial advisors find investments to sell to their clients. Ryan is so good at explaining investments in a visual way that he's constantly asked to give big presentations at various industry conferences—which is great for Ryan: After all, the more he is out there as an investment expert, the more business he gets. Basically, he puts on a fun show while making abstract concepts more concrete.

It doesn't hurt that Ryan is a tall, confident guy with a ton of natural stage presence. But his looks and personality are really secondary to the attention-grabbing props he uses in his presentations. For example, if Ryan is trying to illustrate the unpredictability of financial markets, he might take a little glider, one of those 99-cent balsa-wood toys we all played with as kids, and fly it off the stage into the audience. They watch it make its unexpected loops and turns, buffeted by unseen currents of air in the room, and immediately get what Ryan is saying.

Ryan also manages to sneak some interesting visuals into the PowerPoint presentations his company's marketing department creates for him. Financial industry PowerPoints are notoriously dull, because these firms' in-house compliance departments always sanitize the decks beforehand to make sure they comply with industry regulations. Now, the good folks in Ryan's company's compliance dungeon are there for a reason: to make sure none of their wholesalers go on a wild tear and start advising clients to invest in unicorns that poop gold. (A slight exaggeration, but you get the idea.) The intentions are noble, but the result of all of this extra-careful editing are uniform, vanilla presentations that protect the company from legal trouble but bore the life out of the clients who watch them. It's hard not to keep your eyes from glazing over when you're shown slide after slide of numbers, graphs, and charts.

Don't tell anyone, but Ryan has been known to customize these PowerPoints by slipping in a few photos. Nothing too risky, and nothing that would upset the compliance department—just a subtle image here and there that helps bring the ideas to life. If he is talking about the future, for example, Ryan might slip in a photo of a sunrise. Okay, this might not sound like much. But in a presentation about as visually exciting as dry toast, even a glimpse of something pretty or interesting is enlivening.

POWER POINTERS

A lot of haters come out of the woodwork when you start talking about slide shows, because everyone has suffered through horrible ones. A bad PowerPoint is mind-numbing. (And believe me, in my line of work, I have seen hundreds of truly disastrous PowerPoints.)

But hold on! PowerPoint, or Keynote, or whatever slide show software you use, is a tool, plain and simple. If you don't know how to use a tool, then that tool can be tedious, useless, or dangerous. Give me a chain saw and I'll probably accidentally cut off my own leg. But give me a blank PowerPoint deck and I will weave for you a magically visual journey. You have to know how to use a tool to make it useful.

To take your slide shows from awful to impactful, here are a few simple rules we at Creative Ventures use in our own PowerPoints. Think of this as PowerPoint 101.

- Replace words with images whenever possible. Make each image SIMPLE.
- Choose your images carefully so that they connect directly to the story you are telling. Don't just thoughtlessly throw in any old picture. If you're talking about a retired investor who now lives in a beach house, illustrate that with a picture of a beach house, not a mountain cabin. If you're talking about a man, use a picture of a man, not a woman. You'd think this would be obvious, but it's downright embarrassing how many people slap a random image into a PowerPoint without thinking it through.
- A slide crammed full of words is a presentation killer, so when you do use text, make the letters big. This does two things:

(1) It makes the words up on the screen easier for your audience to read, and (2) it restricts the number of words you can get on each slide, which makes you condense your ideas.

- If you find yourself apologizing for a slide ("Sorry the font is so small," "Sorry there's so much text," "Sorry this graph makes no sense"), then *don't use the slide!* Take it out of your presentation and put the information on it into a printed document instead. ("You'll find all the necessary legal disclosures in the handout I have provided.")

Visual demonstrations aren't just for big meetings. Matt, another master of "They'll know it when they see it," uses visuals to get his ideas across during the intimate dinners where he does most of his business.

Matt, who is based in Massachusetts, is a world-class expert in alternative financial investments. In case you are not a world-class expert in this area, here's an explanation: Standard investments are things like stocks and bonds. Alternative investments are a whole other ball game: hedge funds, managed futures, real estate, precious metals, and derivatives.

These products, though well understood by financial people, are unusual for most of the rest of us. They tend to be complicated; they require high minimum investments and entail high fees. Did I mention the risk is also pretty high? Then again, so is the potential return.

The market for these products is made up of a thin sliver of investors, including institutions (like pension funds) and very, very rich people. Matt makes his presentations to that second, most elusive of groups: high-net-worth individuals with at least $1 million in liquid assets.

Matt deals mostly with financial advisors who manage the portfolios of these superwealthy people. It's Matt's job to persuade financial advisors to get their clients to consider outside-the-box investments. But what makes Matt unusual is that he is as likely to meet with the high-net-worth end customers as he is to meet with the financial advisors who are his official clients. This is because Matt can explain these unusual investments in ways non–finance people can understand. He does this through visuals.

Let's look at one of Matt's demonstrations:

The investment product is gold. Matt is at a dinner meeting with a financial advisor and her wealthy client—the potential investor. Matt's job is to explain why gold is a worthwhile investment. He does this by putting three coins on the table. One is an ancient gold coin from Matt's personal collection, minted in AD 668. The second is a modern one-tenth-ounce American Eagle $5 gold coin (which in 2016 was worth about $140). The third is a chocolate coin wrapped in gold foil.

The chocolate coin, Matt explains, symbolizes the way most people look at gold—as a "fun" material used for treats, like jewelry. The ancient coin is a reminder that gold actually has a very long history of value and worth. Lastly, Matt uses the modern coin to demonstrate that gold is still a viable investment.

Matt then turns the conversation over to the financial advisor, but not before he hands the American Eagle coin to the potential investor and says, "And here's your first investment."

Our last visual virtuoso is Cissy, who's in advertising in Manhattan. One of Cissy's most valuable sales tools is an old-fashioned carpetbag she picked up years ago in a secondhand store. This bag has a floral pattern with leather trim, but the bag itself isn't important; it's the stuff inside its dark recesses that matters. Within what Cissy calls her "bag of tricks" is an ever-changing, head-scratchingly weird collection of objects that seem random at first glance. I laugh thinking about her putting that thing through airport security and then having to explain all the stuff inside to the TSA.

Cissy told me during our interview that she had recently been one of a number of account representatives from various agencies trying to land a potential client in Seattle. This was a packaging manufacturer that wanted to publicize its commitment to the environment. This company had recently pledged to limit the synthetic polymers in its packaging.

Plastic and nylon are examples of synthetic polymers, which are a big environmental problem. These products take centuries to biodegrade and in the meantime impact wildlife and ecosystems. Think of the two million tons of plastic water bottles sitting in U.S. landfills, and plastic six-pack rings strangling sea creatures.

Many of Cissy's competitors had flown to Seattle with storyboards, the standard way of pitching an ad campaign. Cissy came with her giant carpetbag. As team after team went in to make their pitches, Cissy waited, holding what looked like a prop from *Mary Poppins*.

When it was Cissy's turn in front of the prospective client, she set down her bag, introduced herself, and started her pitch. Most consumers, she said, wouldn't understand how important the client's new environmental commitment was until they understood two things: What are synthetic polymers? And how big a problem are they? Cissy said she thought the ad campaign should start by focusing on educating the public about how ubiquitous synthetic polymers are. Then, from her bag of tricks, she pulled out a large pair of panty hose.

I am talking comically large. She asked a couple of the potential clients to hold the waistband, and when they did, they were separated by almost five feet. Everyone in the room gasped and laughed. She explained that this huge pair of nylons represented just one of the zillions of products made from synthetic polymers that would ultimately end up in landfills or oceans.

Just then, an alarm went off. Cissy stopped, reached into her bag, and pulled out an old-fashioned clock, the windup kind with the brass bells on top. She silenced the alarm and set the clock on the conference table. Then she explained that the campaign would have to get across how much time it takes for synthetic polymers to biodegrade. The presentation went on like this, with various props pulled from the bag to illustrate Cissy's points. It was so unusual and imaginative that it led to the hoped-for result: She got the job.

Ryan, Matt, and Cissy are successful because they know a thing or two about the way the human brain, an amazing processor, takes in information. The brain encodes, stores, and retrieves visual information, like pictures and objects, almost 60,000 times faster than it can process words. Visuals are so powerful that companies including McDonald's, Apple, and Nike no longer use their names in their logos. You see those arches, or that apple with a bite out of it, or that swoosh, and, without words, you immediately know exactly which brand it represents. This phenomenon draws on a theory called "picture superiority effect" in psychology research: According to studies, if you show a group of people the word "circle" and then ask them to recall what you showed them seventy-two hours later, about 10 percent of people will be able to do so. But if you show them a picture of a circle instead, 65 percent of them will be able to recall it.

If visuals work for mega-corporate brands and psychological studies, not to mention superstar salespeople, they'll work for you. Use Secret #7 with your clients and they'll know what you mean when they see it.

SECRET #8

W.A.I.T.

"W.A.I.T." stands for "Why am I talking?" Secret #8 is a reminder to **stop, close your mouth, and listen. Listening carefully to your clients is crucial to sales success.** Metrics and statistics and buyer-behavior surveys are useful, but all the research data in the world can't match what clients will teach you if you just pay attention.

Listening to your customers improves your relationships, strengthens cooperation between your team and theirs, and lets you play a role in solving their problems. Help solve a client's problems on a regular basis, and guess what? The client starts to see you as part of his team. Even though you're not an employee of his organization, you basically become an inside member of his conflict-defusing bomb squad. The more you listen, the more you are listened *to*.

Listening fosters deep understanding. Great listeners can determine what is and is not important to a client. They truly *get* the client's issues.

There's a financial payoff to listening, too. Just ask Wayne, a commercial real estate broker in Las Vegas. During a chat with a prospective client, Wayne told me, the client mentioned offhandedly that he'd just had breakfast at a great new downtown restaurant that, the client added, had become a mecca for local business leaders. Someone else might have let this seemingly meaningless side comment go in one ear and out the other. Wayne paid attention and made a note to check the place out. Wayne is now a regular at that restaurant. On more than one occasion he has made a connection there that has led to business.

So listening is important.

The trouble is, it is so hard to do.

"I used to be the worst listener in the world," declared Wayne. "The worst. I violated every element of good listening: I have a short attention span and found my mind wandering as my clients were telling me things. I'd already have a response ready while the client was still talking. I even used to start developing responses *before* a meeting! On the way to a client's office, I'd think, 'I've heard this all before. I know exactly what they need. Let's just skip all this dancing and get to the sale.'"

Okay, that sounds bad. But I am going to tell you how Wayne developed a successful work-around to his natural state of "worst listener" and transformed himself into one of the best.

Wayne is responsible for a phenomenal number of office leases in Vegas. Even when the local real estate market took a huge dive a few years ago, Wayne was still doing a decent business. In his industry, there are agents who represent only landlords and agents who represent only tenants. Then there are agents with the skills to represent both sides.

Wayne is one of those agents, and he is great at it. He might represent an entire office building as well as various tenants who wish to lease space in the building—a situation that, in the hands of a lesser agent, could easily turn into a major conflict of interest.

But Wayne is excellent at negotiating the interests of both sides. A conversation with a prospective tenant might go something like this: "You need the space remodeled? We can do that for X amount of money per square foot. Oh, that's not in your budget? Okay, let me go back and see what I can do." Then he'll present that client's case to his *other* client, the landlord, and wind up with a compromise satisfactory to both parties.

Wayne attributes much of his success to simply paying close attention to what both sides have to say. Remember that he used to be bad at listening? The key words are "used to." "I have become better," he told me. I'll tell you exactly how he did that in a moment.

Kat, too, has become an expert listener. Kat, as you recall, is the pharmaceutical hotshot from Secret #6, Build Your "Like" Platform, who regularly gathers with clients to ask them what they like about doing business with her. If you've gone to the trouble of setting up formal question sessions with your customers, you should definitely listen to and seriously consider their answers. Kat and her team do just that. They have become experts at tuning in.

Like Wayne, Kat also told me on more than one occasion that she wasn't a naturally good listener. In her early days, when she spoke with a client, she would always be a step ahead in the conversation and would often finish the client's sentences. She only became a more patient listener through training and practice.

If you suspect that you're a bad listener, it's not entirely your fault. We humans unconsciously train ourselves to not listen a lot of the time. We are experts at mentally deleting background sounds that would otherwise drive us crazy. We ignore the Saturday buzz of the neighbors' leaf blower. Traffic noise slips by our attention. We hear it but we don't absorb it.

Salespeople are particularly horrible listeners. It's not hard to see why. Sales folks make their living talking about whatever it is they sell. Chances are, the more experienced you are in sales, the worse a listener you are, because you've spent so much time working on your monologue. You probably have a polished, practiced, plus-or-minus-three-minute spiel ready at all times, so that even in a social situation, when someone innocently asks, "What do you do?" they'd better get ready, because your pitch is coming their way.

LIFE'S A PITCH

I dislike the term "pitch" as it relates to sales, because to me, the word implies trickery. After all, in baseball, a pitcher is deliberately trying to eliminate the batter. He's all about deception. A good pitcher is thinking, *How can I fool this guy? Can I blast a fastball past him? Can I make him swing at a huge, breaking curve? Can I hide the ball in my glove so he can't even see my grip?*

These are all necessary strategies in baseball. But in sales the last thing you want to do is trick your customer. Instead of "pitch," I counsel my clients to use "sales story."

Here's the kicker: Sales professionals are all trained to talk, but ask most of them how much training they have had in *listening*, and they'll look at you as if you were a three-headed troll. They simply aren't taught to be attentive. The few salespeople who go from "good" to "great," like Wayne and Kat, have moved beyond talking to active listening.

An active listener is defined by some important characteristics:

- *They are legitimately interested.* Kat genuinely wants to know what people are saying, so she attends to them when they talk. When she is conversing with a client she knows, she often kick-starts conversations around a comment the person has previously made. It's a gesture that shows how closely she pays attention.

- *They concentrate on listening.* Active listening is intentional, not accidental. Active listeners are not doing or thinking about something else and assuming they'll still absorb the important information. Wayne chooses to pay attention through an act of will.

- *They don't interrupt.* An active listener gives speakers space to express themselves, even if that means letting them pause to gather their thoughts. I know: Moments of silence are scary. We desperately want to fill gaps in the conversation with more words about our stuff. Don't!

- *They respond like parrots.* "We do a lot of repeating in our meetings," Kat told me. "We rephrase what a client has said to be sure we understand it," meaning they repeat back what the speaker has just told them, rephrasing the concept in their own words. Doing this ("Let me see if I have this right...") not only helps you grasp the concept but also gives the client a chance to correct you if you have in fact gotten it wrong. It also confirms that you're paying attention.

○ *They ask questions like scientists.* Careful inquiry is a core tenet of science, and scientists are experts at asking probing questions to help them understand something. Look for opportunities to question your client about whatever they're telling you, whether that's serious talk about their business needs or small talk about their kid's college applications. ("When is the lease up on your old office space?" "Where does Junior want to go to school?") Then get curious about the client's answer in order to learn additional information.

○ *They let the speaker know he or she has been heard.* This helps build the connection and cooperation Wayne and Kat talk about.

ACTIVE LISTENING CHEAT SHEET

Active listening doesn't always come naturally. At Creative Ventures, we have been teaching these skills for years, but we still sometimes need to remind ourselves to stop talking. I keep a form handy with key questions that help me kick-start my active listening skills. When a new client contacts my company, I take out a fresh form, ask these questions, and fill in their answers right on the form:

○ Tell me a little about your project.
○ Tell me what triggered this need.

○ Tell me about the problem you are trying to solve.

○ Tell me what the best results of the project would look like to you.

By the way, just to prove I have wholeheartedly embraced Secret #8 in my own business life, I also keep a sign next to my office phone that says "W.A.I.T." It's a reminder, when I'm talking to clients, to speak less and listen more.

But hold on: There's one more fundamental of active listening. In fact, if you do this one thing, you'll be well on your way to a Wayne-and-Kat degree of skill. Wayne told me he became the listener he is today "through one change I made in my sales pitch."

One change. Are you ready to hear it? Are you listening? Here goes:

"I open every interaction with 'Do you mind if I take a few notes?'"

Yep, that's Wayne's magic bullet: note-taking.

In any client meeting, whether he's with a landlord or a tenant, the very first thing Wayne does is pull his trusty Moleskine notebook and ultra-fine-point pen out of his briefcase. These are his listening tools. Through note-taking, he says, "I went from being a horrible listener to becoming a very good, on the way to great, listener."

For Wayne, note-taking tames his wandering mind. When he writes things down, he is able to focus on what his clients are saying and connect to it. It hones his concentration because he is trying to get his clients' ideas on paper.

This was a revelation of near-religious significance for him. Still, "good note-taking was a strategy I had to learn," Wayne told me. "At first I was trying to write down everything my clients said. It was crazy. I was always asking the client to repeat stuff, which, despite my best efforts, made me sound like I *wasn't* paying attention. I realized that I needed a method that worked for me."

Excited at the prospect of becoming a better listener, Wayne looked into how colleges help students become effective note-takers. One big improvement he made was learning not to try to record every word, only the most important ideas. "This was a breakthrough," Wayne said. "It took me from looking down at my notebook all the time to being able to make meaningful eye contact." Once he got the hang of identifying the client's main points, he also was free to glance up from time to time to scan for visual cues, like the client's hand gestures and body language. Another bonus: "The asking permission part lets the client know I care enough to write things down," he pointed out.

Wayne's learned listening skills have paid off in his reputation as a caring broker, and that in turn has paid off in lucrative, long-term relationships and a thriving career. As he put it: "You may have a better product. You may be a better pitchman. But you will never out-listen me!"

Another benefit of W.A.I.T., a million-dollar sales veteran named Duarte told me, is that honing your listening skills will help you avoid becoming the stereotypical pushy salesperson.

Duarte, who works at a boutique financial services firm in Illinois, had his feet up on a conference room table, his hands behind his head, and his tie loosened as he told me how he fell into, and then eventually escaped, the "pushy" trap. Years ago, after graduating with honors from a small Midwestern college, Duarte had jumped straight into sales, which seemed like the fast track to the future he'd hoped for. "I thought I'd make a bunch of dough, control my own universe, and leverage my quick wit and ability to engage," Duarte said in our interview (and after speaking with him at length, I can attest that he does indeed possess these traits).

Duarte's first job was at a life insurance company. After completing the company's sales training program, he hit the streets, raring to go. "I was young and pushing product like crazy. I would start every meeting the way I was trained, by telling the potential client a fear-based story about how they would leave their family destitute without my product. I never listened to a word a client said. I was all push. I thought it was the only way."

Duarte's bulldozer style carried over into his young marriage, too. "I was full of myself. I pushed and pushed in the relationship," he said. "It was my only gear."

But as he moved up the company ladder and began selling more complex insurance products to more sophisticated clients, Duarte found himself starting to get a lot of rejections. It turned out that buyers of fancy insurance didn't like being strong-armed into a decision any more than the rest of us do.

After a while, Duarte left the life insurance business and switched to financial services. The firm he now works for spends hours and hours training its sales force to approach clients in a very different manner. This approach is based on listening. Learning that listening was a key sales skill, Duarte said, changed the way he did his job.

I noticed during our interview that there were long periods when I was suddenly the one doing the talking. Duarte would reposition one of my ten questions so that I would start sharing *my* ideas with *him*, while he in effect became the interviewer. He told me that his goal in every meeting—even in meetings with his long-time clients (and, I guess, with me)—is to listen 80 percent of the time and talk only 20 percent of the time. During his company's listening training, instructors will even use a stopwatch to give salespeople a feel for the passage of time. (This magical 80:20 ratio will make another appearance in Secret #12, Save the Whales.)

By the way, Duarte told me, he has been happily married for twenty-five years now, to his second wife. His first marriage only ended up lasting a couple of years. "You know what went wrong?" he asked. "I didn't know how to listen."

The best sales professionals know that listening pays off in loyal clients and big numbers (not to mention happier marriages). These top performers receive, understand, evaluate, and respond when needed at a level that elevates them above the ordinary salesperson. Remembering to ask yourself, *Why am I talking?* in every interaction takes a ton of practice. But if people like Wayne and Duarte can get better, so can you. If you want to reach the million-dollar club, just W.A.I.T.

SECRET #9

Sell Smart

One of the most comprehensive collections of business books this side of the Library of Congress is in an office building in Houston. The private collection, displayed in floor-to-ceiling shelves with one of those cool sliding ladders, includes books on topics ranging from creative thinking and leadership to accounting. It's very impressive, and if you're lucky enough to have access to it, you can borrow any book you want. Need planning ideas? This collection has books on that. Marketing advice? There are books on that, too.

So how do you get access to this special collection? Do you need a membership?

Nope. You do business with Sharon.

Sharon has built this library over many years at the marketing and advertising firm where she works as a million-dollar account executive. Located in Sharon's personal office, it serves two purposes: One, it's a tremendous resource for everyone who works at the company. Two, it's available to all of Sharon's clients and prospective clients. It's the Sharon Lending Library, a collection of books practically guaranteed to make anyone who reads them better at what they do.

It's a cool idea from a woman with a way-cool job. Sharon and her team will design not just your product's marketing plan and ad campaign but even, if you wish, the product's packaging. It's possible that there are food and personal-care items with packaging created by Sharon in your home right now.

Beyond her unique combination of skills, the other thing that makes Sharon successful is her commitment to learning.

That's where the library comes in. Sharon came up with the idea years ago while brainstorming ways to be more valuable to her clients. It occurred to her that her clients were always looking to become more skilled at what they did. She figured if she could help them do that, well, *that* would be real value-add. Be the salesperson who helps your clients grow professionally and personally, and you become even more crucial to their success than whatever you're selling. The message is: *If you do business with me instead of one of my competitors, not only will you get a great product or service, but I will make you better at your job.*

That's the idea behind Secret #9: **Provide people with opportunities for self-improvement and you'll become indispensable to them.** Note that I didn't say "provide *clients* with opportunities for self-improvement." That's because Secret #9 applies whether you're creating opportunities for your clients or for yourself and your team.

In Sharon's case, her library has become a source of ongoing education for her clients. It's also a built-in marketing tool. Every time a client looks at the borrowed book or uses an idea from it, he'll think of Sharon. It also almost guarantees that he'll have to visit her office at least once more.

I asked Sharon, "How many clients who come to your office borrow a book?"

She smiled and said, "Almost everyone."

"How many return the book?"

She smiled again. "Almost everyone."

That's the sign of a great idea!

LEARN IT OR LOSE IT

The brain processes about seventy thousand thoughts a day. But how does it learn?

The cerebrum, the outermost area of the brain, is the most important part when it comes to learning. It is here that our short- and long-term memories reside. When new information comes in, it gets stored in short-term memory, the brain's central receiving center. Much of this new material is just there temporarily and probably won't make the trip to the long-term parking lot. (Try it: Can you recall what you ate for dinner four nights ago?)

But when we have really learned something, it gets transferred into our more permanent memory bank. Tuesday's pasta and salad might not have made it to long-term memory, but your Social Security number sure has.

Sharon's library took effort to build, but now that it's up and running, it's a nearly effortless way to add value (almost the definition of SIMPLE). Other people I interviewed get more hands-on to help their clients learn new things. I talked to Gideon, a million-dollar hotshot at one of the top global financial firms. He offers his extraordinarily wealthy clients so much more than just standard investment advice. In fact, Gideon has developed his own ongoing series of lectures and seminars, free to any of his clients who wish to attend. "Gideon University" even has its own school crest!

Many of the offerings at Gideon U. have to do with financial topics, such as "Understanding Social Security" and "The Tax Implications of Estate Planning." There are lectures on how to share your financial plan with your family and on the impact of leaving an inheritance to your kids. Should you wish to help with your grandkids' college education, there's a talk on gifting money. Attendance varies, but every offering is a way for Gideon to stay in touch with his clients.

Gideon doesn't teach all of this stuff. He'll often bring in industry leaders to headline. Gideon works out of Chicago, so there are plenty of world-class university professors and experts to choose from. If there is a top economist in town, Gideon will try to wrangle him or her over.

Okay. That's the business side of Gideon University. But Gideon also offers classes on the lighter side. Want to know how to host a lobster boil? Gideon may enlist a chef at a restaurant in town to teach you how. Interested in politics? A local congressperson or city council member will gladly host a meeting for Gideon's clients. Recently, Gideon had a history professor come and talk about Abraham Lincoln; that lecture was booked up in less than twenty-four hours.

Gideon U. isn't an inexpensive or low-effort idea. It involves thinking up and scheduling classes and paying for venues. (Gideon finances it out of his annual marketing budget.) But it pays off. Gideon U. is so much more memorable than client dinners or corporate gifts. Gideon always invites attendees to bring friends who might be interested in whatever topic is being presented. Before every program, Gideon makes a brief pitch: nothing too long or blatantly pushy, but a subtle introduction to a product or an idea. He told me he adds to his client base after almost every class. Whether or not any one course directly relates to finance or results in new leads, each event keeps Gideon at the forefront of his clients' thoughts. It's a genius example of soft touch.

The effort also pays off in gratitude. Through Gideon University, Gideon is actively making his clients' lives better. They recognize that and appreciate him for it. During my interview with Gideon, he pulled out a huge accordion file. "These are all the thank-you notes I have received since I started offering learning as part of my sales approach," he said.

Sharon and Gideon direct their learning opportunities toward their clients. Their message is: *Do business with me and I will help you get better at what you do.*

Ron, who works in insurance sales, uses learning in a different way: to help his *team* become more successful.

Every one of us is a work in progress. We are all in a state of becoming. The best salespeople—the best *people*—never stop learning. Those who put knowledge at or near the top of their list of goals become the best at what they do.

Ron knows this and wants to help every member of the big sales group he manages reach their full potential. He recognizes that a great salesperson needs a lot of different skills, many outside the technical requirements of the trade. To name a few, these include presentation, one-on-one communication, and organizing skills.

Every six months, Ron asks each of his team members to fill out what he calls a "When the Coast Is Clear" report. His people take some time for self-reflection, assess their strengths and weaknesses—both professional and personal—and think about something new they'd like to learn to do. (Sometimes a lot of team members have the same goals; sometimes they don't.) Then he meets with each person one-on-one to craft a learning plan. Ron believes these twice-a-year check-ins are better than yearly reviews, because they keep learning on the front burner.

THE BUFFETT CONNECTION

Ron and I are Parrotheads, as über-fans of singer-songwriter/author/tropical entrepreneur Jimmy Buffett call themselves. The instant I saw the autographed cover of Jimmy's 1978 album, *Son of a Son of a Sailor,* on Ron's office wall, I recognized a kindred soul. Our interview turned into one of the longest conversations of my entire study, and much of it occurred over LandShark Lagers and Cheeseburgers in Paradise at the Chicago outpost of Jimmy Buffett's restaurant chain, Margaritaville.

I bring this up for a reason. Ron's "When the Coast Is Clear" reports are named after a Buffett song of the same title. The song is set in a resort town at the end of summer, after the crowds have all gone home. The person in the song uses this quiet time to take account of himself.

Ron then creates learning opportunities around the goals his team members have identified. If people want to be better at relationship building, Ron might provide breakfast in the office and bring in a psychologist to discuss the topic. If they want to be more efficient, he'll ask an IT expert to demonstrate how the company's technology platform can help them stay on top of their schedules. When the team wanted to brush up on their presentation skills, Ron brought me in. Ron arranged for an ongoing class in conversational Spanish not just for his team but for the entire office: He saw how changing U.S. demographics might have an impact on sales throughout the whole company. Ron also has a whole list of resources he makes available: recommended podcasts, websites, newsletters, and YouTube channels—all filled with information.

Ron has made learning one of the requirements of being on his team. He has created opportunity for each member to grow, expand their skills, and become the best they can be.

So, you might ask, for all of Ron's effort (as with Gideon U., it takes a lot), what is the return?

Every sales professional on Ron's team is either a million-dollar seller or on the way to becoming one. As for Ron, he, too, has gotten smarter and more skillful through the programs he's set up, making him a sought-after expert in his company and the financial industry.

Learning has intrinsic value. Help your clients and your colleagues better themselves, and the payoff will be a better bottom line for you.

GET SMART

While we're on the topic of learning, don't forget to keep learning yourself. The million-dollar producers I surveyed were universally committed to constantly becoming smarter and more knowledgeable. Why? The more you know, the better you can sell.

In a world where change happens at breakneck speed, these pros know that learning must continue beyond their formal schooling. (You know how graduation is called "commencement"? That word comes from "commence," which means "to start." It's a reminder that your lifetime of learning is just beginning.) Learning must go even beyond the continuing professional education you may need to be a certified financial planner, an accredited Realtor, or another kind of specialist.

Our knowledge is transitory and temporary, and as new information becomes available, it's important to keep learning skills you can use to stay educated and competitive and move up the career ladder.

SECRET #10

Get Out of the Office

I was starting to get carsick. Stan was careening around the winding streets of San Francisco, and I was in the passenger seat, trying to take notes. That was the deal. I could interview Stan, but it had to be in the car, in between meetings. Before each of his appointments, he would dump me at the nearest Starbucks, then pick me up again afterward, and I could continue my inquiries. Seemed fair. Stan wasn't the first million-dollar producer I interviewed who encumbered me with conditions.

"Out," he said as he double-parked near a corner Starbucks. I was grateful for the chance to get my land legs back and to review Stan's answers.

Stan was one of the older producers I interviewed. At sixty, he had been at the top of his game for many years and showed no sign of slowing down. Stan sold "professional lines insurance": coverage that protects white-collar advice givers in case their clients sue them. Stan sold insurance to lawyers, accountants, and members of boards of directors; malpractice insurance to doctors; and even cyber-liability insurance, which covers companies in the event of a data breach. Stan had specialized in this niche of the industry for over twenty-five years and knew his stuff.

He also specialized in communicating with clients face-to-face! In a world of instant access, this may seem old-school. After all, we're connected twenty-four hours a day, seven days a week, with the default method of contacting another person being electronic. We text. We e-mail. Instead of shaking someone's hand, we thumbs-up their social media post. Even the telephone is becoming obsolete. At Creative Ventures, we always ask our clients, "What's the best way to contact you?" More and more of them choose anything *but* a phone call.

Sales survey after sales survey backs up the death of the in-person meeting. *It's too expensive*, companies say. *We want our salespeople available.* (What? "Out of the office" does not mean "unavailable"!) According to one statistic I've run across, the average salesperson today spends only 7 percent of his or her professional time in face-to-face meetings.

To which Stan would no doubt say: "Perhaps that's why they're just average."

"I don't get why more salespeople don't build in ample time to see their clients," Stan told me. "But I'm glad they don't. It is a huge advantage for me."

Secret #10 is self-explanatory. In interview after interview, my top sales performers revealed a strong commitment to face-to-face meetings. **Getting out of the office should be part of every sales pro's day.** But the fact remains, it's not.

*   *   *

Unless, that is, you're a sales superstar, like Stan. Or John, a commercial real estate agent in Miami, who uses brief in-person meetings to subtly build emotional connections with his clients. Or Sonny (from Essential Secret #1, SIMPLE), star performer at the Jaguar and Land Rover dealership, who told me he would occasionally visit clients to check up on the performance of their new rides. Since Sonny had a personal relationship with every single person he did business with, he explained, he might go by someone's house, see their car in the driveway, and pop in for a chat.

I have to admit, I was really surprised when Sonny told me this. Why would a million-dollar car salesman take the trouble, not to mention the time, to leave his dealership to go see a client? After all, a car purchase is one transaction in which the customer expects to come to *you*.

But Sonny knew the power of his visits. To him (and likewise to Stan) a face-to-face meeting wasn't a waste of time. It was a deliberate commitment to time, a use of time that top producers say is irreplaceable.

Think about Sonny's visit from the car buyer's perspective: *Wow, this guy cares enough to stop by and check on me.* Where do you think that buyer will go when he or she is ready to buy another Jaguar? When a customer who bought a Land Rover from Sonny is out with his buddies on the back nine at the country club, and they start talking about cars, whose name is going to get mentioned?

That's right: Sonny's. That's why so many of his customers didn't just buy one car from him. Over the years, they bought two cars, or three cars, or had their whole family buy cars from him.

*   *   *

One reason face-to-face meetings are vital to success is, as I've mentioned already, that so many salespeople encounter obstacles that are out of their control. In pharmaceuticals, there's often not much difference in effectiveness between one company's brand-name drug and the generic version, or some competitor's nearly identical alternative. With automobiles, you're fighting product fatigue: There are a lot of different makes for potential buyers to choose from. In real estate, clients may have a limited choice of properties to lease or buy, but they have an almost unlimited choice of brokers they can work with. With all of these variables they can't manage, the salespeople at the top of these industries focus on what they can control.

As Armande puts it, "It's easy to cancel a contract, but it's harder to cancel a relationship."

Armande, who specializes in leasing space in big, beautiful office towers, calls face-to-face meetings "the superglue of my sales process. They hold everything together." His product, office space, is essentially a commodity. "But I am unique," Armande says.

What makes Armande special is his customer service, and he uses face-to-face meetings to remind his clients of that. Armande treats meetings as what I call "emotional ping points"—brief moments of reconnection.

Now, these face-to-face meetings don't have to take a long time. Sonny's were very quick "soft touch" meetings in which he might hand his customer a coupon for a free oil change, or the

124

latest issue of *Car and Driver*. Stan's meetings went a little longer, because they were usually about specifics. ("We've made some changes in our coverage you might want to take advantage of.")

Armande "pings" his clients by arranging to stop by their places of business for very quick updates. He might be there to discuss the customized walnut cabinetry going into the conference room in their new headquarters. He might be there to recommend a moving company with which he has negotiated a discount. Yes, he could conduct some of this business over the phone, but he chooses to take the extra step and do it in person. These little pings cement his relationships. Brilliant!

PING!

Sonar is a way of locating objects by sound. Send out sound waves, wait for the waves to hit something, and they'll bounce back, telling you where that something is. The military uses it, and so do bats.

Austin, Texas, where I live, is home to as many as 1.5 million Mexican free-tailed bats that live in a huge colony under the Congress Avenue Bridge in the middle of town. Every evening during the summer, the bats fly out from under the bridge in a huge cloud in search of bugs to eat for dinner—to the delight of tourists and locals, who use the spectacle as an excuse for a nightly viewing party. (In Austin, there's always a party.)

Bats navigate by sound. As they search for insects, mostly mosquitoes, they make noises we can't hear. But when these sound waves hit a bug, the bat knows where supper is. Bats may not see very well, but they are experts at pinging their surroundings. As you "ping" your clients, remember that you're doing it to remind your-self that they're out there, and vice versa.

Armande, Stan, Sonny, and other great producers who regularly get out of the office understand intuitively what researchers at MIT have discovered about human interaction in face-to-face meetings. When you get together in person, you take in all kinds of sensory information you can't pick up on a conference call or through text or e-mail. Communication is not just what your client is expressing verbally; it's also his or her conscious and unconscious body language. Armande told me, "When I am with my client in person, they first see *me* and then my product. If I contacted them any other way—if I relied on only electronic touch points—they would see the product first and me second." If Armande does his job right, *he* is the face of the deal, not the gleaming glass facade or the ultramodern reception area.

True, not every product or service demands this special in-person attention. And some customers will stay loyal to a company or brand regardless of what kind of service they get. Armande told me, "Some people will only buy Apple products or only drink Dr Pepper" (aha, a man after my own heart). But in the competitive world of office space, he went on, "my money is on the relationships revolving around me."

"Get out of the office" is such rookie advice that you'd think it would be part of every salesperson's day. (It's another example of the Duh Factor, which you first heard about in Secret #6, Build Your "Like" Platform.) But the fact remains it's not standard practice, which means that the salespeople who do follow it are automatically in the superior position.

If you are in a line of sales that truly doesn't allow for face-to-face meetings, or if your company places more value on its employees being at their desks than on results, it's possible that you'll need to leave that company or at least work to get yourself promoted into a position that allows you to leave the building. To help make that happen, work on your interpersonal communication skills (Essential Secret #4, Make Friends First, and Secret #8, W.A.I.T., are good places to start), and your presentation skills (see Secret #7, They'll Know It When They See It). If you work as a support person for a higher-up salesperson, ask your boss if you can accompany him or her on a few face-to-face meetings, just to watch. If a job eventually opens up, you'll be ready.

And to really benefit, you must do face-to-face meetings well. The secret to a successful in-person get-together is not just landing the appointment in the first place or picking the right spot for lunch. For great producers, it's research. In Sonny's case, he might have asked during a visit, "How's your car performing?" But he'd already know the answer, because he would have checked the vehicle's service record in advance.

As Stan put it, "I can't waste my client's time or I won't get that face time again." He laughed and added, "Most of my competitors do their preparation on the ride up in the elevator."

GET READY FOR YOUR CLOSE-UP

No top sales pro goes into a face-to-face meeting without planning for it ahead of time. I collected these tips during my interviews:

Who is this person? How much do you know about the individual you're meeting with? Go through the drill: Google. Facebook. LinkedIn. The more you know about "Jada" or "Jeremy," the better equipped you'll be to have a productive conversation—which, by the way, is certainly sure to happen when two folks hang out in person. If your client's profile includes photos of fighter jets, it might be that he has a military background. If you see that she volunteers for the ASPCA, and you happen to have just adopted a rescue puppy, have a snapshot of your dog at the ready, just in case.

Who does he or she work for? Your client likely represents a larger organization, so knowledge about that organization comes in handy. How is the company doing? Are its financials solid, or are profits only a distant memory? Is the organization known for making purchase decisions quickly? How is the company perceived in the market? Is it a traditional firm or a place you'd read about in *Wired*? By the way, it's good to know all of this about *your* company, too.

How much time does your client have? Time is a really big deal. Value your clients' tight schedule, and they will value you. Let them know in advance how long the meeting will last, and then stick to it. If the client wants more time, he or she can choose to extend the meeting.

What is the plot? A "plot" is different from a "plan." A plan is a detailed proposal for achieving something, like closing a sale. A plot is the reason for your out-of-the-office meeting. There needs to be one, even if you're just casually dropping in for a moment to ask about a client's car. Keep in mind that this is sales time, and if you don't have a legitimate reason for seeing someone face-to-face, or can't gin one up, you've just wasted your own time. *I'm going to stop by and say hi to Jeremy* is not a plot. *I'm going to stop by, drop off a coupon for a free carwash, and say hi to Jeremy* is.

What other meetings can you fit in today? As Stan and I hopped from one face-to-face to the next, I realized: Great salespeople schedule their out-of-office days like military generals, taking advantage of time and geography. They fill these days with activity, one meeting flows into the next, and they always have a plan B. If one of Stan's clients cancels on him at the last minute, he'll likely have a backup person in the same office he can ask to go see instead.

What are you wearing? Mark Zuckerberg can get away with a hoodie. But for everyone else, corporate sales has a distinct uniform, and that uniform is probably a suit—whether you're a man or a woman. Dress for success.

Great producers get out there. They fill up freeways, trains, and airports all over the country. So should you. Think about it: You need relationships to build your business; you need to be connected on levels beyond just the product or service you're selling; you need your clients to need you. Can you get all that from clicking away at a keyboard? No. Understanding the importance of personal contact and using it in the sales process is one of the great differentiators between the average salesperson and the extraordinary salesperson. Even in our global village, you need face time. You need to shake a hand. You need to see a smile. You need the human touch!

SECRET #11

Charm the Gatekeepers

"Pizza is only fifty dollars."

"What?" I asked.

"For fifty bucks," T.C. said, "I can feed my client's entire support staff."

T.C. (his name is Thomas, but he goes by his initials) had just finished placing a lunch order to be sent to the office of one of his customers. Two days earlier, T.C. had hand-delivered a simple invitation to this client's receptionist, Maggie, whom T.C. has known for years. He knows about Maggie's husband and her family, that she is a huge music fan, and that her kids live for football. He also knows that Maggie will serve as his town crier, spreading this news around the office: "Nobody bring lunch on Wednesday. T.C. is sending pizza for all of us."

T.C., a financial services wholesaler, has been treating his clients' support staffs to regular lunchtime pizza parties for five years. It's his version of a tactic many of my interviewees use: **When building sales relationships, million-dollar producers don't just focus on the decision maker at the top of the ladder.** They also spend time and attention on the people on the lower rungs: the receptionists, assistants, secretaries, and other gatekeepers who manage access to the executive with the purchasing power.

Gatekeepers take their responsibility very seriously, and if you're in sales, you likely have developed some strategies to circumvent these people. There are books, articles, webinars, and classes based around sneaky ways to "bust through the gatekeeper," "bypass the gatekeeper," and execute other maneuvers that sound like tactics you'd study at West Point. Gatekeepers are viewed as the main impediment to making a sale. Many salespeople see them as the enemy.

And there are *a lot* of gatekeepers. Think about all the people you have to deal with before a decision maker ever signs that purchase order. I can tell you this: It is never just one. Even if, through some miraculous twist of fate, you started the sales process with the final decision maker, you will still have to negotiate with legal folks, buying agents, administrative representatives, and almost certainly the assistant or receptionist who works directly for the decision maker. That's a lot of people between you and your paycheck.

If you view these people as impediments, though, you're starting off in a pretty combative frame of mind. You dread making your sales call, thinking, *I've got to figure out how to get that assistant out of the picture.* So what if, instead of viewing gatekeepers as barriers to crush or obstacles to make an end run around, you made friends with them?

T.C. had the inspiration to start his pizza parties after hearing that pizza restaurants seldom did a great business at lunch. Armed with this information, he met with a small, family-owned place in his town and offered them a deal. T.C. would order a certain number of pizzas every week if the restaurant would give him a discount on these orders. (Typical of T.C.'s preparation: He explained how the restaurant could increase its business by sending coupons to each office, along with its delicious pies, so workers might come in on their own sometime.) The pizza joint owners jumped at the opportunity, and the relationship has been steady ever since. Sometimes T.C. just has pizza sent over to an office; other times he delivers it himself and joins a staff for lunch. Thanks to T.C.'s regular gestures of kindness, you can bet his calls always get put through.

"Look out for number two" starts with reframing the gatekeepers in your mind. That's what Kelly, another one of the highly successful pharmaceutical salespeople I spoke with, does. "First," she told me, "change the way you are looking at the people between you and the sale. They aren't a *barrier*; they are a *filter*. They're part of the sale." Kelly recognizes that there are a lot of people involved in any sales relationship and that these folks don't live to stop her from doing her job. She doesn't even consider them minor players. "There is no 'second level' to me," she says. "Each person is part of the bigger whole."

With that mind-set, she sets out to work *with* them, not against them.

Kelly works in the Northeast, making sales to clinics and hospitals with not just one person, like Maggie the receptionist, to get past, but with layer upon layer of gatekeepers. There are people who block access to decision makers in almost every department, and many of these people, who usually work in support or administrative positions, don't even know that one of their roles is to be an obstacle between a salesperson and the decision maker. They just know they're there to guard their boss's time. On top of that, hospitals are huge bureaucracies. Kelly told me, "The levels below the actual buyer are very chaotic and, at best, a challenge to define. I have to deal with a whole lot of gatekeepers as I construct a sale."

Kelly's philosophy helps her avoid the frustration that can come from having to get past so many different people. It makes her job a lot more pleasant. She doesn't dread sales calls; she enjoys them, because she is making and dealing with friends.

Just how do you work this magic?

"You'd better have a strategy," Kelly said.

Here is hers:

Begin at the beginning. The first gatekeepers you're likely to encounter are receptionists. Get to know them. In fact, Kelly advises, "spend a disproportionate amount of time getting to know them," without even thinking about the many rungs of the purchase ladder above them. Kelly is on a first-name basis with most of her clients' receptionists, and when new receptionists are hired, she learns their names right away. A receptionist might not seem like the most important gatekeeper to you, and he or she likely has no direct say in whether you make a sale. But, says Kelly, "There is real value when I walk in the door and the receptionist says, 'Hi, Kelly!' " When you are on a first-name basis with a gatekeeper at any level, you're more likely to be treated as a friend.

Create a lineup card. Kelly compares the hospital and clinic staffs she does business with to baseball teams, and she has stats on each player. She uses information she gathers through online research, phone calls, and in-person meetings. She keeps track of the players (in pencil, because the lineups constantly change), with meticulous notes next to each one. She reviews the lineup card before every visit. That way she, too, can call staff members by their first names.

Be polite to absolutely everyone. "I once had a CEO tell me, 'The reason you are sitting here is that you were so nice to everyone on my team,'" Kelly said. "I tried to remember anything I had done special, but in hindsight it was simply being respectful." An ordinary salesperson might not realize that treating every single person well is one of the best ways to ensure that every single person treats *you* well. Think about this the next time you want to yell at your waiter because your food is cold. Who do you think is the last person between that reheated plate and you?

Listen. If you want the gatekeepers on your side, learn to pay attention to what they say. "Every person on the team is filled with information," Kelly said. "I learn more about the right pathway to a sale by listening than anything else I do." (For more on listening, see Secret #8, W.A.I.T.)

Kelly has the right idea: Win over your client's support staff, and you've got it made. The process takes time, "but a large hospital is a sales gold mine," she says. "It is worth the time investment if I get a single product sale. That single product is the entry to our entire catalog of medications."

E-MAIL JUJUTSU

"E-mail Jujutsu." I love that term. I heard it from Marti, a real estate agent. Jujutsu is the Japanese martial art of close-in sparring. Marti uses it as a metaphor to describe the phenomenon in which one e-mail leads to another, which leads to another—exhausting rounds of back-and-forth communication that start to seem like grappling matches. Marti, though, is an expert in the smart deployment of e-mail, especially to support staffs. For example, if an e-mail string exceeds three rounds, she will stop the string and make a call. She keeps her e-mails to no more than three sentences, because she knows short communiqués tend to get read and answered more quickly. Some other tips to avoid the e-mail struggle:

- *Don't use e-mail to sell.* Remember, most of the time you aren't e-mailing the buyer or the decision maker but that executive's support staff. Don't use it to make a long pitch. Instead, use it strategically to get to the next level of the sales process.
- *Copy everyone.* Unless an e-mail is confidential, cc everyone on the support team so that they feel involved. If they want to opt out, they will tell you.

Your decision maker's support staff aren't the only gatekeepers to consider. To demonstrate how to manage a different kind of guardian, I give you Trey, a Mercedes-Benz salesman who has been working in the business all his life. He learned everything he knows from his dad and landed his first job as a kid washing cars at his father's dealership. He never looked back. "All I ever wanted to do was to sell cars," he told me. "Even as a kid, I could see the excitement in a client's eyes when they drove that new car off the lot."

Now, you might be thinking that maybe Trey is in the wrong

chapter. Why would anyone have to deal with a gatekeeper in a car sale? Well, just hang on: Trey does fit in here.

"You might be surprised by the number of couples who come in looking for a car," Trey told me when I interviewed him. Making a deal with a pair of buyers—let's assume a husband and wife—calls for an entirely different strategy than dealing with a solo buyer. That's because, as Trey puts it, "there is always a No in a couple. One of these two people will be the decision maker, and the other will often try to talk the decision maker out of his or her choice." That's especially true, he says, when the choice is going to cost $50,000 or more.

So Trey starts to manage the second level the minute that couple walks into the showroom, starting with his greeting. He says hello and introduces himself. He shakes both people's hands. "Forget about thinking of them as a man and a woman," he says. "They are potential lifelong friends and, more importantly, lifelong customers."

MAY I HELP YOU?

"My dad taught me never, ever to open with 'May I help you?'" Trey says. Wise advice. *Everyone* needs help in a new-car showroom. Trey uses, "Welcome to our dealership."

Banning "May I help you?" from your greeting is a good idea in pretty much any sales situation. When you ask someone if she needs help, that's a closed-ended question. She can immediately answer no. Once the potential buyer turns down your offer of help, you're at a disadvantage.

Next, Trey simply listens, allowing the buyers to tell him their story. Soon enough, he can identify who is the decision maker and who is the (either supportive or obstructionist) partner.

Then he starts working to make that partner happy. "My dad told me never to attack an objection. Instead, ask one simple question: 'Can you tell me more?'" Trey said. "If you listen, in their objection you might find the next step."

That next step might surprise you: Sometimes a couple will come in dead set on a certain model, like a sedan, and end up leaving with something completely different, like a sporty two-seater. This isn't a surprise to Trey, though. He knows that buying a car is not just a practical purchase; it's also an emotional one. "I have learned that if I do a good job listening to both parties, I give them the flexibility to change their mind," Trey says. His goal is to help them find the Mercedes that leaves the decision maker with that huge smile, and to involve the second level in the decision enough for, at the very least, a grin.

Great sales performers like T.C., Kelly, and Trey thoroughly understand that a sale is made up of layers of people. They construct relationships that go beyond just the decision maker. Stop thinking of the gatekeepers as a nuisance, give them the attention they deserve, and you'll learn the value of being called by your first name.

SECRET #12

Save the Whales

Humans might be at the top of the food chain, but *Balaenoptera musculus*, aka the blue whale, is the true Goliath of planet Earth. No living creature in the history of our world, not even the dinosaurs, can compare in size and scale to the blue. Its heart alone weighs a thousand pounds. Its low-frequency song can carry for miles beneath the waves, making it the loudest animal on the planet.

Perhaps not surprisingly, top producers call their most important customers "whales." Whales are the largest and the loudest clients, the ones who bring in the most money for you and your company. Whales are the "20 percent" in a formula called the 80/20 rule, which posits, in a nutshell, that 80 percent of your business comes from 20 percent of your clients. **Save the Whales means that you should spend more time and attention on the big clients in that top 20 percent than on the smaller fish in the bottom 80 percent.**

THE PARETO PRINCIPLE

The 80/20 Rule, also called the Pareto principle, is the brainchild of Vilfredo Pareto, an Italian economist who came up with the formula in the 1890s while studying wealth distribution in Italy. Pareto realized that about 80 percent of the country's wealth was in the hands of only about 20 percent of the population. Although the Pareto principle is not a scientific fact, there are examples of it across many different fields:

- In his studies of quality control in manufacturing during the mid-twentieth century, the management consultant Joseph M. Juran found that 80 percent of product problems were caused by 20 percent of product defects.
- In 2002, Microsoft found that 80 percent of the crashes in its Windows and Office software could be traced to about 20 percent of all the system bugs it had detected.
- Pareto even discovered while growing pea plants in his garden that 20 percent of the pea pods produced 80 percent of the peas.

The appeal of the 80/20 rule is that it provides a rough guide to where you should put your energy and focus. If 20 percent of your clients are responsible for 80 percent of the dollars in your pocket, then they also should get 80 percent of your resources and attention.

I got to see this in action when a financial services superstar named J.J. invited Creative Ventures to present a storytelling program called "Why We Love the Movies" at a private event for his whales. It was a weeknight in Austin, and J.J. and his family-owned boutique business had rented out a local movie theater and dressed it up like a big Hollywood premiere. There was a red carpet. There were spotlights. Local actors were dressed up as famous stars. The firm sent limousines to pick up attendees from their offices, and everyone got their picture taken holding a pretend Oscar. This evening of film and fun was no small soiree, and it was just the most recent in a series of client events the office hosts every quarter. There have been golf outings, wine tastings, cooking classes—all to thank the top 20 percent of the office's client base for being such great customers.

J.J. is his firm's top producer, with annual sales that put him in the highest echelon of the industry he works in. And J.J. has always recognized the value of his deep-pocketed investors. "They are my best of the best, the people who create my success," he told me as we stood at the entrance to the theater. He pointed out one of his whales. "That client is responsible for introducing me to three other clients who are also here," he said. "Each is worth their weight in popcorn and Pepsi."

J.J. is pretty smart. He sees these parties as a way not only to thank the whales but also to get all of them in one room at the same time, so they can benefit from meeting each other. "There's a big advantage to letting them rub elbows," he said. "They see these functions as not only great rewards but also as opportunities to network." J.J. also benefits: It takes less effort for him to throw one big thank-you celebration for a lot of whales than to entertain each whale individually.

This idea of ranking clients and rewarding the best ones has been around as long as sales—and as you've already read, sales has been around for a long time. Airlines, retailers, and even coffeehouses separate out the biggest spenders and lavish them with seat upgrades, bonus bucks, or free lattes. As a sales professional, you or your company likely already use a process called segmentation, categorizing accounts by the amount of money they bring you. You might have A, B, and C-level clients or platinum, gold, and silver clients. No matter what you call these groups, the idea behind segmentation is twofold: First, it motivates smaller clients to do more business with you in order to achieve VIP status. Second, it lets VIP clients know their current (and future!) business is recognized and appreciated. The ultimate goal is to develop lifelong customers who wouldn't think of going anywhere else for the service or product you provide.

The first step to Save the Whales is to figure out who your whales are. Likely, you already know. Sales departments track this sort of information, and it's the rare salesperson who isn't well aware of exactly who their best customers are. If you don't know, for heaven's sake, drop this book immediately and go ask your boss.

Great producers can always answer these key questions:

- Who are my clients?
- What does each one spend on my product/service?
- Which ones provide the highest streams of revenue?

In addition to these basics, there was not one million-dollar salesperson in my study who could not name their whales' likes,

142

CLIENT RELATIONSHIP SECRETS

dislikes, and personality traits. I often tested my interviewees' understanding and knowledge of their whales by throwing questions at them. Let's say a salesperson started talking about a big client named, say, Maria. I would start the grilling process:

- What color is Maria's hair?
- Where does Maria live?
- Is she married?
- What's her spouse's name?
- Does she have children?
- What are the kids' names?
- Tell me something really interesting about Maria.

I can't remember any interviewee who couldn't answer every question I threw at them. They had intimate knowledge of their whales, gleaned from a strong and profitable relationship. That knowledge led to the next step in their plan: figuring out how much it would cost them to assure the whales' continued business. What would be a good investment of money, time, resources, or all three? And how much more would it take to get more out of them?

Now, deciding to lavish more attention on a few clients might seem heartless to you. After all, there are only so many hours in a day and only so much money in your budget, and if you're giving more love to a small group, by definition you're giving less love to a large group. The next step toward mastering Save the Whales is to get over the guilt and allot your resources wisely.

Meet Elizabeth, a financial services wholesaler who works in a beautiful campus-like setting in Seattle. Elizabeth, aka Liz, is an 80/20 rule expert. "I know who my top dogs are, and I treat them accordingly," she told me.

Like all big-number sales producers, Elizabeth knows where every nickel she makes comes from. While she's committed to all her customers, she'll readily tell you that the whales get special treatment. She has a "top client" calendar separate from her business calendar, on which she marks her whales' birthdays so she can send them warm cookies and milk (yes, this gourmet delivery service exists). She marks the first anniversary of each whale's first significant purchase and commemorates the occasion. She donates Thanksgiving dinners to needy families in her whales' names.

For a while, Liz told me, she had to fight against her belief that all customers are created equal. During her early years she adhered to this emotionally generous idea, but eventually she realized that it didn't make strategic sense. Assign a little more importance to her best clients, Liz realized, and they would not only continue to buy her company's financial products, they'd also likely buy additional products and introduce her to new clients. Keeping these clients at the center of her world would open doors to new opportunities.

Liz calls this her "low-hanging-fruit strategy" and says it pays off in bountiful sales. "But it took a long time," she told me, "to understand the difference between equal and fair."

As I spoke to top salespeople about their whales, I would often hear, "There isn't a problem I wouldn't solve for them." If a top-20-percent client needs assistance, million-dollar producers will find a way to drop what they're doing to help the client out. If it means staying up late or working through the weekend—*done*. If it means jumping on a plane—*done*.

One reason my interviewees have time to lavish attention on their whales is that the very state of having a few gazillion-dollar accounts means you don't need as many accounts overall. With fewer clients competing for your time, you can focus on those who fit your target profile. A financial services star named M.J. made that point when I spoke with her. Her roster of high-net-worth clients are well worth the effort she spends dreaming up ways to keep them happy.

(Okay, actually, she told me, she "steals" a lot of the ideas she learns from other salespeople at industry conferences, then modifies their ideas to fit her own style and market. And why *wouldn't* she do this? Conferences are events where top salespeople share their best sales strategies. She never passes up the opportunity to listen, and neither should you.)

Some of M.J.'s whale bait includes:

The "Support Suite." M.J. has assembled an all-star roster of business connections, advisors, and top-drawer service people she's always happy to put her clients in touch with. These include CPAs, estate planners, attorneys—even college admissions experts for those clients with college-bound kids. Not only do her clients have easy access to a prescreened list of helpers, they also enjoy special pricing. After all, each of those all-stars desperately wants to be on M.J.'s list; it means that they'll be recommended to a whole host of potential clients with very deep pockets. So M.J.

is able to negotiate discounted fees. This, of course, makes M.J.'s whales very happy: The funny thing about super-wealthy people is that, just like the rest of us, they love a deal.

The Gathering. This sounds like a meeting of a coven of witches, but it's really an elite annual get-together M.J. and her firm's other salespeople plan for their very top clients. Each year they invite a handful of whales to a different sports event: the Masters golf tournament, the Super Bowl, the Indianapolis 500. The Gathering is one of M.J.'s most successful ideas and a critical whale-saving strategy.

Giving together. M.J. gets involved in her elite clients' favorite charities, a great idea that lets you give back while bringing you closer to your clients. One of M.J.'s whales is actively involved in the American Heart Association, so M.J. sponsors a table at the nonprofit's annual gala. She also donates items to auctions and participates in 5K walks for the charities her clients support.

Big clients are golden. They generate a large volume of sales. They refer you to their wealthy friends, who become new big clients. They're worth the effort and the expense to keep them happy. Don't be afraid to spend 80 percent of your time and resources on them.

ROYAL TREATMENT ON THE CHEAP

In Las Vegas, whales are elite high rollers who give no thought to slapping down hundreds of thousands or even millions of dollars at a casino. Not surprisingly, to entice the big players through their doors, Vegas resorts go to great expense to lure them in, even sometimes paying for private jet transportation to and from the casino. But special treatment doesn't have to cost a fortune. Some of the cleverest sales superstars I interviewed bestow royal status on their whales in very low-cost, low-effort ways:

Color code. When a client reaches a certain investment threshold, one financial services guy moves the client to what he calls the Purple Group. (The color purple has connoted royalty since well before Queen Elizabeth I forbade anyone but the royal family to wear it; historically, purple dye was rare and costly.) A client's purple status begins with a "Welcome to the Royal Club" letter sealed in purple wax, and an excellent bottle of wine in a purple velvet bag. The purple theme continues thereafter: Top-client dinners have purple linens, and their reserved seats at sporting events are marked off with purple ribbon.

A regular reminder. One advertising agency stays at the top of its whales' minds by enrolling these important clients in a monthly gift delivery service. Depending on the client's level of business, the delivery might be a magazine subscription, a tea of the month, or a gourmet food basket. It doesn't really matter what the gift is; what matters is that it suits the individual client's taste and provides a monthly reminder of his or her relationship with the agency.

SECRET #13

Not So Fast

I need it yesterday.

Time is money.

Get on this right away.

You hear this type of thing constantly in business, a world in which speed sometimes seems the only goal. Start-ups must "grow fast or die slow." At Facebook, a longtime motto was "Move fast and break things." And when it comes to organizations in general, the prevailing wisdom is that "small equals fast and big equals slow."

I get it. Speed is a strategic tool. And I know most of us have no patience for anything that takes time, whether that's waiting for a video to stream or baking a potato. (Although I don't agree that "big equals slow." If you do, you might want to race a Saturn rocket against a Mini Cooper.) But I want to tell you: Despite everyone's obsession with *faster*, **the superstar salespeople I interviewed almost universally make it a point to slow down their sales process whenever they can.**

Why? Because, if you remember, when you're a million-dollar producer, nothing is more important than your relationships with your clients. And nothing can screw up those relationships like letting speed outweigh thought—prioritizing *I have to do this now!* ahead of *How do I do this in a way that serves my client at the highest and best level?* I've said it before and I'll say it again: Million-dollar producers are in the relationship business.

Don't get me wrong: You can't completely ignore the importance of speed. If your client has needs, you should of course take care of them as quickly as possible. But how quickly? That depends. In a rather unusual survey result, the producers I spoke with were divided on the issue of speed and when it's important. The difference comes down to: What are you selling?

If you are selling *stuff*, then speed is often a necessary way to stand out from the competition. One good example is Amazon.

Amazon has mastered speed. It can recommend a book or electronic gadget in the blink of an eye; it lets you buy the thing in one click, and two days later a guy in brown shorts is setting that purchase on your porch. In some places your order can even arrive in a couple of hours—although, unless you're buying a tourniquet, I'm not sure what you'd need that desperately. Even when you're buying basic items, like vitamins, Amazon makes it easier (not to mention cheaper) to shop on your iPad than to run to the local stick-and-brick pharmacy or big-box store. Amazon proves that "speed" and "stuff" are a match made in heaven.

But if you're selling a product more consequential than vitamins, or a complex service that needs more setup time to position properly, well then, slow down a little. The algorithms at Amazon may be great at telling you what you want to buy before you even know it, but there is no algorithm for relationships.

If you work too fast, you make mistakes, which you then have to correct. That sets you back a few steps, which means you need to rush to get back on track, which will probably mean you make even more mistakes. Before you know it, you're stuck in permanent recovery mode. It's a vicious and exhausting cycle, and it will eventually cost you clients.

Great producers are great at recovery, but they are even better at stopping those mistakes from happening in the first place. They do that by slowing down when necessary.

MISTAKES WERE MADE

People mess up—even the best of the best. When my interviewees discover an error, they don't make things worse by rushing in to fix it. Instead, they slow down long enough to answer two key questions:

1. What caused the error?
2. How do we correct it so that the client's needs are met?

Sometimes the issue is fairly simple to solve, in which case they go ahead and communicate with the client that they've made a mistake and explain how they're going to rectify it. But if the problem is more complicated, they take time to decide on the best way forward. While they're off figuring out how to fix the error, they don't just disappear. They make the client aware of the mistake the moment it happens and say, "We'll be back in touch shortly with a solution."

Brandy, who works in Austin, is an Olympic gold medal-level residential real estate agent. She single-handedly sells an average of sixty homes a year. She has been named a Five Star Real Estate Agent, an industry designation given to only a handful of professionals who deliver extraordinary customer service five years in a row.

The lady can sell houses.

She also knows all about the need for speed. In fact, almost every buyer and seller bombards her with demands for fast service:

"I'm relocating next month and need a home ASAP."

"We're in town for one day and want to see as many places as possible."

"I want to list my house now, and I need a quick sale."

Brandy can do things quickly. Remember, she closes on an average of at least one home a week. But she's also working to provide the award-winning customer service she's known for, and a lot of her new buyers and sellers have been referred to her by former buyers and sellers. One of the things people who have worked with Brandy tell their friends is that she is a full-service agent. *Go with Brandy*, they say, *and she will take care of everything*. Every piece of paperwork will be accounted for; every appointment will be on time; every shingle will be inspected. Brandy's clients love her because she's thorough.

But being thorough takes time. Brandy's challenge is to move quickly without sacrificing any of the service details that make her stand out.

So how does she deliver consistently good service in a timely fashion?

By being extremely organized in ways her clients don't see.

Before Brandy meets with a new client, she told me, she has already started the sales process. Because so many of her new clients are referrals, "one of my happy customers has already set the table for me ahead of the first meeting," she said. "More often than not, that client will call me and say, 'Hey, Brandy, I recommended you to our friends the Smiths, who are looking for a home.' I'll ask the referring client two questions: 'What did you tell them about me?' and 'Tell me a little about the Smiths.'"

Brandy asks those two questions to kick-start her sales process. If she already knows the Smiths are looking to downsize to a smaller home, for example, she can gear her first meeting toward that.

Once she's working with a new client, Brandy's system really kicks in. Buying or selling a home is a complex transaction with a lot of moving parts. It can involve mortgage brokers, insurance agents, building inspectors, escrow specialists, and lawyers. Brandy streamlines the process for her clients by helping with these details. She might send a client an e-mail that says, "Here's the phone number of the mortgage insurance company I recommend. Ask for John; I prepped him for your call." She makes it easy and fast.

Brandy is able to do this because she has automated most of her own tasks (that e-mail, for example, is scheduled and prewritten). Her brilliant behind-the-scenes structure lets Brandy focus on making every client feel important, even as she whisks them through a complicated transaction. It gives her time to spend an entire day with a buyer looking for just the right home. Without this system in place, she would be hurried and disorganized, wasting the client's time. Definitely the wrong kind of speed.

Brandy has internalized an important lesson: Even though her clients want to buy or sell as fast as possible, urgency is not really what drives her business. It's her attention to detail during the entire process, from hunting for a home to moving in, that makes her so special. Provide a Brandy-level of service and clients will fall in love with you. You can't forget entirely about the need to hustle, but the key is to hustle while still giving customers more than they ever dreamed of.

Ellen is another highly respected and awarded real estate professional. She has not closed on a property priced at under $2.5 million in over ten years. In the San Francisco Bay Area, where she works, prices like this are the norm: San Francisco has the highest share of million-dollar houses in the United States.

There are fewer potential buyers for properties that are extremely expensive. So some buyers, knowing offers on a specific property may be few and far between, try to force anxious sellers to act quickly. *If you don't respond to my offer fast*, a buyer will imply, *I might just walk away.*

Ellen knows this. She also knows that the quickest way to destroy a sale is to hurry through it. Miss a detail and the whole deal could fall through. So Ellen has created a secret speed bump in the sales process—a cool-your-jets procedure to slow down fast-racing buyers or sellers without their realizing it. She calls this "the loop."

You know the loop: that information cycle so many of us seem to be "out of." If you're in the loop, you know what's going on. If you're out of the loop, you don't.

If you're working with Ellen, you can be sure she'll keep you in the loop. In her first meeting with a client, Ellen maps out every step that has to happen before a sale can be finalized: securing a loan, arranging for inspections, and so on. (She actually draws a loop that begins with that initial meeting and ends with the house becoming a home.) She also asks the client to choose how they would like her to keep them in the loop, whether that's by e-mail, text, or phone. That makes the client accountable for keeping up with whatever information she needs to communicate to them.

The main purpose of the loop is to help her clients understand the process. But Ellen also secretly uses it to manage her clients' expectations of how fast each step will be completed. She might tell a client, as she's sketching out their loop, "You may want this inspection to happen ten days from now, but you need to be aware that it'll be two weeks." Down the road, if a client is frustrated that it's taking two weeks to get that home inspection, Ellen simply refers to the loop, reminding them that the deal is still on schedule. The loop doesn't stop every speed-obsessed client from throwing an "I want it now!" tantrum, but it helps.

Jeff, a transportation insurance wholesaler, uses a similar idea to buy time when he's trying to put together a complicated deal. Jeff works as the middleman between big insurance companies and the agents who match individual clients to the right policy for their situation. Sometimes agents get stumped and can't find the specific kind of coverage a client needs. Enter Jeff.

Jeff knows everything about transportation insurance, which is specialized coverage for commercial vehicles. All of those things you see on the road—buses, eighteen-wheelers, taxis, rigs that haul hazardous materials—require insurance. Some of that insurance is very complex, and your average agent might not know which insurance product will meet a particular client's needs and which companies sell it. Jeff does.

In insurance, "fast" is a common demand. An agent might call Jeff and say, "I have a limousine company that needs coverage today, because they're picking up Mick Jagger at the airport tomorrow." Jeff uses a great little trick that slows down the panicked agent, allows Jeff to visualize exactly what the agent is asking for, and ensures that Jeff doesn't get so caught up in solving the problem *right now* that he misses a crucial detail:

He sketches out a diagram of the agent's request.

In his desk, Jeff keeps blank copies of a type of diagram called a spoke and wheel. As the agent describes what his client needs, Jeff begins to fill in a template with crucial facts. He jots down the name of the client seeking the insurance (say, a large farming concern), any extenuating circumstances (maybe a bad claim history), the client's existing policy, and the budget.

This formal exercise helps Jeff to slow down and take the time to think and solve these complicated problems. His thought shows in his performance, and his insurance agent customers come back to Jeff again and again to fill their clients' trickiest insurance problems.

Brandy, Ellen, and Jeff have developed the discipline and the methods to slow down, think, and create the absolute best outcome for every client. They balance the need for a fast sale or a quick answer with the understanding that going too fast can lead to relationship-jeopardizing mistakes. Want satisfied clients who stick with you over the long haul? Then slow down enough to do your job right.

— *Part III* —

Work Performance Secrets

Harness Your Energy,
Get Organized, and Manage
Your Schedule Like a Sales Superstar

SECRET #14

Embrace the Dark Side

"What's that?" I asked Roger, pointing to a wall in his office. Facing the desk was a huge floor-to-ceiling bulletin board covered with three-by-five index cards in a rainbow of colors, each card filled in with carefully printed notes.

"Oh," said Roger, who's in financial services on the East Coast. "That's the Wall."

The Wall, it turned out, was a collection of every "No," "Wrong product for me," "Not interested," and "I already work with someone else" answer Roger has ever received from a potential customer. Turn down Roger, and your reason goes on the Wall, immortalized in the largest shrine to negativity I have ever seen.

"The Wall is my motivation," Roger explained when I asked him why in the world he would have that depressing thing in his office. "It's my notes on what to do differently. It's my strategy to combat rejection. It's my ultimate learning tool."

About thirty minutes into our interview, there was a knock on Roger's door and another sales associate popped her head in.

"Sorry for the interruption," she said. "I was hoping to take a look at the Wall."

Wow, I thought. *These people have really embraced the dark side.*

Not too many careers come with as big a dark side—so much negativity and rejection—as the one you're in. When you interview for a sales position, you're far more likely to be asked how you'll handle the disappointment of not closing a deal than how you plan to spend your bonus check. Every organization understands that a few rounds of No can destroy even the most promising young producer. No is intimidating and demoralizing and makes you want to give up. You might think if you hear No one more time you will cease to exist. In the universe of sales, No is the dark energy that threatens to rip the whole thing apart.

Meanwhile, Yes is as rare as intelligent life in the universe. Life is unusual. Life takes a lot of stuff happening in just the right amounts and the right order. Life is fragile and rarely evolves quickly enough to survive. Life is kind of like closing a sale.

With No so common and Yes so rare, it makes a weird sort of sense that a top salesperson like Roger would try to find a positive use for all of that negativity. But Secret #14 goes deeper than that. **Embracing the dark side means accepting that No will happen far more often than Yes will, and figuring out how to use that inevitable rejection to your best advantage.**

Roger and his team members make a point to study the endless variations of No that they hear, to help them rehearse counterarguments that might get them to Yes the next time. They use the Wall to rehash each disastrous situation so that if it ever comes up again, the team will be prepared—as in, "If a client objects to _____, I will explain it like this: _____."

All of that darkness is formalized right there on the Wall. And, far from being demoralizing, it is inspiring and useful. Nothing else Roger has ever done has benefited his career more than the Wall. He uses it to get even better at his job.

Embracing the dark side isn't easy. Roger told me it took years for him to recognize that every failed sale was a learning experience screaming in his head: *This isn't the last time you'll hear this particular excuse. The next time, you'd better know how to answer it.*

"I'm not sure," Roger told me, "but I would be surprised if anyone else spends as much time on their mistakes as I do. In my business, sometimes just using the right sentence at the right time will make the difference. I know this, because here are all the times I used the wrong combination of words."

"It's these little things," Roger added, "that give me a true competitive advantage."

THE "SMALL" DIFFERENCE
BETWEEN WINNING AND LOSING

Little things matter. Success can come down to the smallest details. For proof, consider auto racing.

In races like the Daytona 500, the winner is often determined by the narrowest of margins. Races last for hours, but the car that crosses the finish line first sometimes gets there just moments ahead of the rest of the competition. The number two driver might be behind the winning driver by a mere second and a half.

Are the tiniest details that important? Ask the driver who crosses the finish line in second place.

The idea that your failures have worth is something the greats learn early in their careers if—and I do mean *if*—they are paying attention.

Remember Mary, my insurance client's Salesperson of the Year from the introduction of this book? Well, Mary really is a phenomenon. Now retired, she was in commercial insurance for over twenty-five years and rose to top producer status at every company she worked for. At her last company, she held that title seven times.

Mary was one of the longest interviews of my entire study—not because she was a talker but because she was a treasure trove of knowledge. In fact, we'll meet up with Mary a couple more times before this book is over. She is *that good*.

At one point during our interview, Mary started talking about how often she was met with rejection and how she was able to cope with it. Mary had learned to accept No as part of her job. In fact, she told me, she expected No because only after a certain number of times hearing No would she finally hear Yes.

She said, "Here's what's important, and I am shocked at the number of salespeople who don't know this—including my peers."

Then she gave me some statistics. They go something like this:

- Almost half of salespeople give up on a prospective customer the first time the customer tells them No.
- Of the ones who try again, almost a quarter give up after the second rejection.
- Of the salespeople who try a third time, about 15 percent give up after the third rejection.
- And of the handful of diehards still in the ring, a little more than 10 percent give up after the fourth rejection.

Basically, if one hundred salespeople pitch the same customer, after four rounds of that customer telling them No, only one of them will be left. If you think of it that way, who do you think is going to make the sale?

The one still standing.

That is embracing the dark side.

WHY YOU ARE EXACTLY LIKE GEORGE CLOONEY

Most actors face a constant, soul-crushing flow of No. When they audition for a job, they hear every possible rejection: You're too old, you're too young, you're too blond, you're not blond enough, you're just not right for this aspirin commercial (or whatever). It's hard not to take that personally and to get bogged down in negativity: *I'm not talented enough; I'm a loser; I blew it.*

Back before he was a superstar, when he was enduring rejection like every other auditioning actor, George Clooney had an insight that helped him embrace the dark side. He realized that directors held auditions because they were trying to solve a problem. They had a role to fill, and they needed someone to fill it. If he was rejected for a part, it probably wasn't because he was a bad actor but because he wasn't the right actor to solve the director's problem.

Sales calls are very similar to auditions. You are selling yourself, your company, and your product or service. As with auditions, No is always in play. It's helpful to remember, as Clooney learned, that sometimes you just aren't the right person with the right product or service to solve a customer's problem. Accept that and move on.

Another interesting thing about negativity: It's not just a sales phenomenon. The buying world has its own dark side. Great sales professionals understand that often, No stems from a client's fear.

Your clients are afraid of screwing up. They're scared of change. They worry about taking a chance and failing. They fear looking stupid. When a client is afraid and has to make a quick decision, it's often just easier to say no, even when saying yes might be in their best interest.

Here are some of the things your client is thinking as you make your sales pitch:

- *If I don't make this purchase, I'm toast.*
- *If I do make this purchase and it doesn't work out, I'm toast.*
- *If I don't buy and my competitor does, I'm toast.*

Almost no matter what they do, they end up cooked bread.

The good news is, you can use your buyer's fear to your advantage.

Clint, who is in advertising and marketing in Houston, has learned exactly how to do that. Before pitching his services to a prospective new account, Clint dreams up the absolute worst *Titanic/Hindenburg* thing that could happen to the client's business if they *don't* hire him to handle their advertising and marketing. This disastrous potential outcome is always based on the client's doing nothing. How might the competition beat them? How might their business fail to grow?

Clint then creates a storyboard (that classic advertising visual) around this worst-case scenario. In exploiting this fear of the unknown, he's like the first chapter of a Neil Gaiman book.

Also, he pretty much does away with the possibility of hearing no during his first meeting. In fact, during this meeting, Clint doesn't give the client an opportunity to say no, because at that point they have nothing to say no to. Clint isn't pitching them his services—yet. He is simply showing them the possible outcome should they choose to continue down their current path.

One of Clint's accounts was a successful car dealership. When Clint pitched them, the dealership was getting ready to open a second location—this one on Car Row, a strip of the city with numerous already-established auto dealerships.

The first time Clint came in to meet with them, he did not present one new marketing or advertising idea. Instead, using a series of drawings, he laid out the nightmare scenario. First, he reminded the prospective client of how much money they would be spending to set up shop, acquire inventory, and staff up at their spinoff location. He then showed them how not investing in appropriate advertising could backfire. He described the long, difficult journey to gaining market traction and set out drawings of what their dealership might look like: its sales staff milling around idle, row after row of unsold new cars sitting in the sun.

He then sat back and waited.

The prospective clients began to bombard him with worried questions.

Clint already had the answers, of course, but he didn't say anything. He let the scenario sink in and told the client he would be happy to show them some simple, powerful, and creative marketing and advertising solutions—at their next meeting.

Three days later Clint presented his marketing plan. The client hired him the same day.

If you've ever ridden a roller coaster, you know there is a very small space between "Oh, no!" and "Oh, yeeeaah!" The same is true with the distance between No and Yes in sales. Great producers thrive in this gap. They understand that No is a daily part of life. When you use planning to leverage that No—when you start embracing the dark side—you can turn it into Yes.

SECRET #15

The Ten Times Rule

I was kind of mindlessly watching a baseball game on TV, checking into and out of a game that didn't mean a lot to me: Red Sox versus Reds. Then something happened that caught my attention. With the Red Sox's Yoenis Céspedes at the plate, the Reds' pitcher Jonathan Broxton let loose a sizzling fastball right at Céspedes's head.

With reflexes honed from years of experience, Céspedes miraculously dodged that ball by a fraction of an inch and threw himself out of the way. Coming so close to a shattered jaw might have rattled a lesser player, but Céspedes regrouped, stepped back into the batter's box, and smashed the very next pitch into the center-field seats for the go-ahead home run.

WOW. Céspedes didn't let that nerve-racking moment impact his goal. In fact, the pitch might have steeled his resolve to show Broxton who was boss of the plate. Tenacity, determination, and good old-fashioned grit got him back in the box, swinging for the fence.

Hitting a baseball is really hard, and calmly hitting a home run after the pitcher has just tried to brain you is even harder. Sales is really hard, too. *Really hard.* There are hundreds of thousands of people out there peddling everything under the sun. The ones who thrive must internalize the Ten Times Rule. I'll get to why I call it that in a moment. **First, Secret #15 is about perseverance, sticking it out, standing tough, and staying the course in the face of setbacks.** Most people don't possess this ability. But all million-dollar producers have it—and it can be learned. If Secret #14, Embrace the Dark Side, is about accepting that at some point in your career—and probably more than a few times—you will stand at the edge of a deep, emotional well of failure, Secret #15 is about the grit you use to yank yourself out of it and keep going.

Now, I'll explain why I call it the Ten Times Rule. I named it in honor of Mary, one of my favorite interviewees, whom you've met several times by now.

In the last chapter, Mary explained that she had weathered a monsoon of No during her career. She eventually realized that, in sales, you only get to Yes after some amount of No. So she began keeping track of how many Nos it took to get to Yes, and she came up with the number ten. That's right: Based on her past experiences, she realized she generally approached a potential customer an average of ten times before finally making a sale.

It was a brilliant coping strategy. Once Mary figured out that she'd almost certainly be rejected a whole bunch of times before she was successful, the rejections stopped bothering her. In fact, she simply began *planning* to approach each prospective client ten times. After all, if you know most clients will tell you No ten times before they say Yes, then you stop worrying about the fourth No, since you realize you'll hear five more of those before you make the sale.

This is the Ten Times Rule: You're going to have to keep trying, over and over, in order to be a superstar seller.

The Ten Times Rule, by the way, is kind of a companion secret to Essential Secret #2, The Jordan Formula. The Jordan Formula describes all the behind-the-scenes effort it takes to come out and give an effortless-seeming superstar performance. The Ten Times Rule is a reminder that this effort must be long and sustained—and systematic. If you want it to pay off, you have to resist the temptation to quit. Many of Major League Baseball's great hitters practice their own form of the Ten Times Rule. They'll wait at the plate patiently, letting foul-off pitch after foul-off pitch pass them by, looking for *their* pitch—the perfect one to hit. It is a process. The more pitches they get to see, the more likely they will get that pitch they are looking for . . . and the next thing you know, you hear that classic crack of the bat signifying a hit.

Now, the name "Ten Times Rule" is just a name. I am not claiming that ten is the scientifically proven number of times you must face rejection or try at something before you succeed. The name just means that, in order to be a superstar at anything, you have to persist in the face of rejection for quite a long time. The number itself—whether it's ten thousand hours or ten Nos to one Yes—is not as important as the idea that success takes the focused decision to not give up. Following the Ten Times Rule also means you must take the attitude that sales is really hard work.

THE POWER OF TENACITY OVER TIME

The Grand Canyon is a magnificent sight to behold. It runs over 270 miles in length. At its widest, it's eighteen miles across. It is over 6,000 feet deep. To give you some idea of its scale, all the water from all the world's rivers could fit into the Grand Canyon and still only fill it halfway.

Yet the Canyon was created by a single stream of water, the Colorado River, cutting its way through rock for millions of years. One stream of water running in the same direction.

Sales is kind of like the Grand Canyon. Your chosen career takes a single line of focus around many repeated steps. Hard work, resiliency, the willingness to go at it over and over to achieve a result. Sales is a stamina business, and building your million-dollar career takes grit. Nothing can replace that element in your success.

By the way, the Grand Canyon gets bigger and deeper every day!

For Leo, another interviewee, the Ten Times Rule was more like the Seven Times Rule. Leo figured out this formula, he told me, only after making a huge career mistake. As with many decisions, history points toward outcome, and in Leo's case that arrow had been pointing the wrong way.

Leo had been a very successful financial advisor in Philadelphia. He had a multimillion-dollar book of business made up of executives in a specific sector of the economy: His investors were owners, presidents, and other C-suite leaders in a wide variety of American manufacturing businesses. The idea of cultivating a niche client base—in Leo's case, manufacturing executives—is always brilliant. But that's not really Leo's story.

Because Leo was so good at what he did, he ultimately succumbed to a prevalent belief in sales culture: If you are a great salesperson, you will be an even better sales *manager*. Nearly every corporate sales department has had the bright idea to yank a great producer out of his sales role and promote him into management. That should work, right? I mean, a guy or gal who excels at selling a product should be able to transfer that acumen to managing a team of people, right? Companies figure the rest of the team will flock to a successful salesperson who has had skin in the game—who has been there and done that, and done it well.

The trouble is, selling things and leading teams of people are completely different skills. Great salespeople traditionally have little or no management experience outside of managing their own client relationships. They are really only experts in leading themselves. This doesn't mean some salespeople don't become great managers; it only means that often they don't realize they're making a mistake by taking these positions. Dangle a VP title and a steady salary in front of a salesperson, and many are more than willing to hand over their client lists and head to the corner office.

Leo certainly was. The idea of sharing in a team's compensation was so enticing, he gradually transferred his clients elsewhere and went from superstar producer to so-so manager. Leo now says it was a horrible mistake. He readily admits he "sucked" at management. He was so unhappy, he eventually quit.

Leo wandered around for a while looking for his next opportunity. He couldn't get his old clients back, because his contract had a noncompete clause. In order to build a new book of business, he'd have to start from scratch with a whole new crop of clients. Leo was still an outstanding asset manager and knew that if he could find new clients, he could have a successful career again. But he'd have to start cold, like a rookie salesperson. And as you know, starting cold means persisting despite a ton of rejection.

You have probably already figured out that if Leo wound up in this book, he did in fact rise again to become a million-dollar producer. And you're right! The plan he developed to find new clients turned out to look a lot like the Ten Times Rule.

First, Leo researched all the manufacturing companies within a one-hundred-mile radius. He identified the leadership trust at each place and eventually, like hard work disguised as magic, he had compiled a cold-call list. Most of these people had never heard of Leo, but he had researched their businesses and could identify their investment needs. Remember, Leo knew this stuff like the back of his hand.

Then he had to start contacting them. This is the part of the sales process that is particularly demoralizing and difficult and requires vast amounts of perseverance. To get himself through what he knew would be a long slog of trying and, in many if not most cases, failing to score meetings with these prospects, he planned to contact each prospect multiple times over the course of a few weeks. Basically, he was doing what brand-new, beginning salespeople have to do: targeted prospecting.

- Contact attempts 1, 2, and 3: three blind e-mails. Each time, Leo introduced himself, summarized how his background and success might fit with the prospective client's needs, and requested a meeting.
- Contact attempt 4: phone call. If Leo wasn't lucky enough to get to speak with the prospective client, he would leave a message introducing himself and following up on his e-mails.
- Contact attempt 5: fourth e-mail. "I am going to be in your area on the following days and have these times open. Would you be interested in meeting to discuss investment opportunities?"
- Contact attempt 6: second phone call. "Just touching base about my e-mail. Would you be interested in meeting? If so, what's the best time to get together?"
- Contact attempt 7: final e-mail. "I am sorry if my persistence was off-putting. It appears that my background and expertise do not fit your current needs. Please know that, should you wish to be in touch in the future, I am always at your service."

What is instructive about Leo's career comeback is that he developed a specific formula to follow. It was the kind of process Leo was familiar with, because he had done it so often in the past. Defaulting to the familiar made perseverance a little more comfortable for him. When his confidence eluded him and he was tired and discouraged, he stuck to the formula. Leo would probably tell you that he doesn't have any superhuman reserve of tenacity; instead, when the going got tough, he just did what he knew how to do. The lesson here is that you don't have to be born with grit. You can plan in advance for how you'll summon it when you need it, so that you can fake it if necessary. Attitude can carry you through even the toughest battles.

NEITHER PEACEFUL NOR EASY

Jackson Browne: Going Home, the 1994 documentary about the rock legend, includes a story I love about grit and hard work. It's from Don Henley of the Eagles, who describes how Browne taught him an important lesson about songwriting. As the story goes, in the early 1970s, before these guys were famous, Henley lived in the apartment above Browne in the same Los Angeles complex. Henley describes hearing the same distinct, repetitive melodies wafting up from Browne's apartment as his neighbor played them on the piano over and over and over again. Henley would thump on the floor, hoping to get Browne to play something else. But Jackson was working on writing "Doctor My Eyes," and crafting songs takes repetition. As Henley noted, songwriting is a job.

Like sales, songwriting is process-driven. The search for a melody is like the search for leads. The repetitive process that generates a hit song is no different from the process that generates a sale.

Leo's method took a lot of perseverance, but it was his version of the Ten Times Rule. Rebuilding his career took planning, tenacity, and the refusal to view obstacles or rejection as a personal failure. He just had to keep going.

This persistence, the willingness and grit to keep at a task despite setbacks and annoyances, is a common trait among super-successful people, including sports heroes, rock stars, and billionaire entrepreneurs. Grit has to do with your attitude. It is about passion for one's long-term goals. It's about putting ego aside for the sweat and tears of the process. It's about almost getting smacked in the face with a fastball, gathering your composure, and hitting a home run.

Although grit seems to be a naturally occurring trait of successful people, it actually can be created. Put a well-thought-out process in place and follow it with determination, and you will make your own grit. Fend off disappointment with focused activity, and you'll have grit, just like Leo did. Discover your own Ten Times Rule and the end result will be grit.

At the beginning of a sales career, success is about volume; it's a numbers game. The more touch points you generate, the more likely you are to get a sale. You are given a quota of calls to make, and if you follow these numbers with effort, you will start to build business. You are given a script and told, "Get to it." You spend countless hours calling people who don't know you; your company name might keep your prospect on the line for the first fifteen seconds of your call, but that's about it. Then you start to understand that selling is a very personal business.

You also rapidly learn what boxing champ Mike Tyson meant when he said, "Everyone has a plan until they get punched in the mouth." You realize you're in the punched-in-the-mouth business. If you have grit, though, eventually you'll start to see a little progress. You make a few sales. You get glimpses into a future where you might actually have a career. You start to learn perseverance and develop a protective shell against negativity. You begin to figure out which efforts yield the best results. You develop systems and processes; you reconnect with successful clients and get referrals. You become a sales professional.

"I'm in the setback business," Mickie said, describing the term. "I make gains and then something happens. The market changes, the availability of money lessens, or perhaps my key contact changes jobs and I have to start a relationship over again."

Mickie, who is based in the South, makes a fantastic living selling insurance to corporations, but not without a lot of hard work and, yes, setbacks. She and her team need to contact each prospect somewhere between six and twelve times to turn the prospect into a prospective client, and even then there's no guarantee that hard work will pay off in a sale. "Imagine you have done all the e-mails, phone calls, and face-to-face meetings—when you can get them. Imagine you have done all of that," Mickie told me. The next step is to put together a coverage plan. "You sweat through all the clients' requirements and all the regulations, put together a proposal, and feel you are in the driver's seat." Even then the client can say no.

"Now, that's an emotional and economic setback," Mickie said.

The reason Mickie doesn't let this destroy her is because she knows that, despite it all, she will end up winning more than enough deals to make up for the ones she loses.

Mickie, Leo, and Mary are excellent salespeople. But beyond their talent, luck, brains, and skill is the quality of persistence, of grit, and of plain sticking it out. Their willingness to try, and try, and persist for as many tries as they decide is necessary proves that they have mastered the Ten Times Rule.

SECRET #16

Master the Day

Percy runs a lucrative financial company with exactly one employee: Percy. He is an independent insurance salesman, a retirement specialist who helps elite businesspeople protect and grow their savings to ensure a comfortable future. He has spent thirty years building this empire, which he runs from his home in Santa Fe, New Mexico, one of most beautiful little corners of the country.

As an independent business owner, Percy is responsible for every element of his one-man operation, from mundane tasks like bookkeeping to traveling ten days a month for the key face-to-face client meetings that are at the heart of his practice. You can imagine the challenge of running a specialized financial services company and being responsible for absolutely everything. How does he get it all done? Why does he not get bogged down in the little details?

Because Percy is the master of his day, that's why.

Master the Day means "Do your most important work during your most productive periods." Master the Day means *you* control the use of your time, and your time is your most valuable asset. Million-dollar producers like Percy know this. They guard their time and energy ferociously, without apology, so they can direct it toward the activities that matter most to their success.

Master the Day starts with recognizing your own individual energy pattern. Do you know yours? Some people reach peak energy before lunchtime. Some hit their stride just as everyone else is hitting the hay. Some people have multiple daily peaks and valleys of energy. And then there's the huge crowd of people who have no idea what I'm talking about—who have never thought about what times of the day they're most energetic.

There's a lot of power in identifying and taking advantage of your daily energy pattern. If you know when you tend to be at your best, you can schedule your most crucial work during these times. Tap into your energy and you'll be much more productive.

Percy, like me, is a morning person. He'd say he's at his best between 6:00 a.m. and noon, so he programs his workload so that the critical stuff, like making financial decisions on behalf of his clients, is done within these hours. The rest of his workday, which usually ends around 3:00 or 4:00 p.m., he spends doing the less important stuff. During this low-energy period, he might work on expenses, do research, or book travel for his road days.

Percy hardly ever schedules calls during the afternoon hours. Why? Because he's tired by then, and he knows that being at the peak of his energy during conversations with existing or potential clients is of utmost importance. His clients understand this, too, because he makes sure to tell them. Most know not to call him on a regular basis for financial advice at two in the afternoon, and they're fine with that. If a large hunk of your future depended on Percy, you'd want to catch him at the top of his game, too.

PLOT YOUR ENERGY

Even if you're sure you already know the best and worst times of day for you, it's worth taking the time to make an energy map. This exercise will help you gain clarity and direction. It's easy and, yes, you actually should do it:

1. Pick a specific time frame to track: One workweek is good.
2. Decide on the span of time each day you'll be tracking. We usually recommend 6:00 a.m. to 9:00 p.m.
3. Create a three-column chart. (We like old-school notebooks, or use a spreadsheet if you prefer.) Label the columns "Time," "Energy," and "Task."
4. Set an alarm for hourly check-ins. When your alarm goes off every hour, record the time, what you have been doing, and how energetic you feel. Use a simple 1-to-5 point system, with 5 = I could jog to the moon and back and 1 = I am barely functioning.

At the end of the week, make a graph. Label the X (vertical) axis "Energy." Label the Y (horizontal) axis "Time." Plot the graph with the data from your worksheet. You'll quickly see the ups and downs

Gertrude—okay, don't *ever* call her Gertrude; it's Trudy—learned early in her illustrious career that there was never enough time to get everything done, but there was always enough time to get the important stuff done as long as she learned to focus and harness her energy.

An agent at one of the largest residential real estate firms in

184

the United States, Trudy is a master at focus. For her first few years in the business, though, she was a time victim. Every workday was interrupted by a litany of distractions: phone calls, unexpected meetings, e-mail notifications, a staff member popping in to talk—things you are probably familiar with. And, like most people, most every time, Trudy would stop what she was doing and flip her attention to the interruption. It drove her crazy. Not only did she not get what she needed to done, she lost her focus so completely that whatever work she did manage to accomplish was pretty inferior.

Trudy's company understood the value of sales productivity and sent her to a series of time-management workshops, where Trudy learned some great ideas. But when she tried to apply them, they didn't make her typical day much less insane. It turns out it wasn't *time* Trudy needed help managing. (Time already has a management system: clocks and calendars.) What Trudy needed was *focus* management. She asked herself, *How can I be the most productive?* and came up with the answer: *Don't try to do two, three, or ten things at once.*

Try time blocking, a disciplined approach to productivity that divides the workday not by hours but by activities. Or, as Trudy calls them, "events." Time allotted to reading and answering e-mails is an event. Time allotted to making and returning phone calls is another event. Time allotted to budgeting is yet another event. A sales meeting, a home showing, even her workout—each of the activities that fill up Trudy's days—is an event.

Trudy divides every workday into hour-long pieces and then allocates one of these pieces (or half of a piece, or two or three pieces) of her workday to each of the events on her plate. She uses a paper calendar and diagrams these chunks of time using colored squares to represent the pieces of the workday. She fills in the squares with whatever assignment she has given herself. Then, during each allocated block of time, she does what she has planned and nothing else. If Trudy's workday is eight hours (actually that would be an easy day for her), she creates eight segments into which all the elements of her day must fit. Each evening before she calls it quits at the office, she juggles and re-arranges the blocks for the next day. Trudy alternates between high-energy and low-energy tasks so that she doesn't get stuck doing the important things during times when she's not in top form.

On any given day, Trudy's calendar might look something like this:

- 7:00 a.m. She arrives at the office, coffee in hand.
- 7:00 to 8:00 a.m. She reviews the news of the day so she can talk about it with her clients and team. Trudy sub-scribes to a few newsletters and looks at relevant web-sites, making notes on anything important. She values being informed, and this quiet time lets her enjoy her coffee and get herself in a more energetic frame of mind.
- 8:00 to 8:15 a.m. She reviews the day's agenda.
- 8:15 to 9:00 a.m. She jots down anything she wants to discuss at the "Daily Huddle," a mandatory, ten-minute-tops "state of the union" meeting that happens every Monday through Thursday and keeps everyone

in the office apprised of what is going on that day. (See sidebar.)

- 9:00 a.m. to 9:10 a.m. Daily Huddle.
- 9:10 to 10:00 a.m. Trudy tackles her e-mail.
- 10:00 to 11:00 a.m. She makes and returns phone calls.
- 11:00 a.m. to noon. Trudy researches home sales and new listings with an eye toward properties that may interest her clients.
- Noon to 3:00 p.m. This is Trudy's high-energy period, when she goes out with clients.

There's one more way Trudy keeps her mind on only one activity at a time: She makes it clear that there are certain blocks during her day when she is not to be disturbed. When she's in her office and needs to get through her phone calls and e-mails, she closes her door and puts up a sign on the outside that says FOCUS TIME. People know not to interrupt her when the sign is up, unless it's an emergency. The focus time concept extends to her meetings with clients. When she's out showing properties, she silences her cell phone. Trudy will never take a call when she's with a client. The client gets her full attention.

HUDDLE UP

Communication comes in all shapes and sizes, but one of the most important aspects is flow. Some communications come in blasts or as single elements, but great sales producers need a different kind of access to information. At Creative Ventures, we created a SIMPLE way to communicate that's used by many of the professionals in this study to help keep everyone in that legendary loop.

The Huddle is a planned, daily group meeting—yep, every day. It's short—between five and ten minutes. It happens in the morning, usually first thing. People huddle either in person, on a conference call, or via FaceTime or Skype. There are never more than three items on a Huddle agenda.

The Huddle is a disciplined team strategy that keeps everyone up to date on the day's key information without taking away any sales time. Try it!

It takes discipline to stick to the time-blocking method. (A beginners' tip: Using an alarm can help you keep track of when each block ends.) But for Trudy it pays off. She and her team are one of the most productive groups within their entire organization, and Trudy went from being sent to time management workshops to giving them! She is often asked to speak about her time-blocking system at company meetings and national industry events.

AVOID THE MEETING TRAP

I could write an entire book on what's wrong with meetings, those productivity black holes that suck the life out of everyone.

The way it usually happens is, you are in the zone, doing your work. Then it's meeting time. The meeting is scheduled for an hour.

There are five people in the room, which means that this hour-long meeting is really a five-hour meeting, because each person there has been taken away from something else. Each will also need time after the meeting for follow-up and to get up to speed again on whatever he or she was doing before.

Meanwhile, there's a good chance that the meeting will have no agenda. Nothing gets decided; no schedule is set; no projects are assigned.

If you are the person scheduling the meeting, for heaven's sake, have a hard start time and a hard stop time (which for a morning meeting could be when the donuts are gone) and a clear idea of what you want to get accomplished.

If you are the one invited to the meeting, you aren't crystal clear on the meeting's purpose, and you have enough seniority that you won't be seen as presumptuous or not a team player, try asking the following, so at least you can come prepared:

○ May I please see the agenda?
○ What would you like my contribution to be?

Trudy and Percy understand the value of protecting their energy. The rest of us seem to be slowly but surely killing ourselves while doing our job. We think nothing of fourteen-hour days. We try to work past our breaking point. We may know intellectually that extra hours aren't necessarily productive hours, but nevertheless we miss sleep, eat a bunch of crap, and get little or no exercise because we think that "more" is the goal. It isn't. Just a reminder (see Secret #5, One Level Above): "More" doesn't automatically mean "better." And "better" doesn't mean "best."

Now, Master the Day may not come as easily to you as it does to Percy, Trudy, and other experienced salespeople who have risen after many years into senior positions. The more successful you are, the more latitude your higher-ups will give you to program your workday, but if you're not there yet, controlling your own day can be more challenging. You're kind of at the whim of what your higher-ups want you to do. And, of course, being his own boss gives Percy more freedom than he would have even if he were a top producer at a larger organization.

But to make it to their level in the first place, you'll need to own as much of your day as you're able. At the end of every workday, you should feel like you've directed most of your energy toward whatever is most important to you. Identifying, harnessing, and valuing your energy will help you get to your goal faster and more efficiently.

SECRET #17

Make Your Own Metrics

The religion of sales is measurement. Salespeople worship at the altar of data, numbers, and benchmarks that give you an objective view of how you're doing. The industry's obsession with measuring performance approaches that of baseball.

WHO'S ON FIRST

Technological advances enable us to crunch more numbers faster than ever. This is no truer than in baseball, which has been obsessed with metrics ever since Abner Doubleday's first pitch turned into a pitch count.

Even if you are not a fan, you probably know what RBI and ERA mean (if not, that would be "runs batted in" and "earned run average"). But baseball long ago entered the measure-everything realm. The futuristic system Statcast uses technology such as HD cameras and radar to an obsessive degree.

If you want to know the exit velocity of a home run, no problem. If you'd like to know the degree of spin on a curveball, you've got it.

If you're curious about the acceleration of the diving center fielder as he makes a *SportsCenter* highlight catch, it's here.

Obsessive measurement is alive and well in Major League Baseball.

It makes a lot of sense. Sales has always been and always will be about tangible results, which should certainly be measurable. And in business, as the saying goes, *if you measure it, you can manage it.*

But consultants also have a saying: *By measuring everything, you measure nothing.* **Secret #17 is about paying attention to the data that matters to you.**

This isn't easy for most salespeople, who suffer from statistical overload courtesy of their employers. In business's quest to measure everything, salespeople are subject to an endless deluge of raw data. Companies love to dump massive and overwhelming amounts of it on their sales forces. There's nothing helpful about having an avalanche of data dumped on you. And for people who don't like to keep track of data, it does seem that the list of sales metrics continually expands, limited only by management's imagination and its ability to actually quantify the thing in question. Companies measure revenue generated per salesperson (a biggie), lead response time, pipeline opportunities (aka potential sales), appointment ratios, conversation rates, cost of sales to revenue (aka how much do they have to spend to get a sale), and sales cycle timelines. Oh, and give the measurement a name that leads easily to an acronym and *boom!*—you get ACV (annual contract value), AMRR (average monthly recurring revenue), and

CAC (customer acquisition cost), not to mention FAB (features, advantages, and benefits), OKR (objectives and key results), and probably numerous other things yet to be invented.

Meanwhile, every salesperson is also required to provide a ton of data to the boss: the number of sales calls you make, the percentages of products you sell.

If you're like most salespeople, you hate this aspect of sales culture. It's micromanagement, it drives people nuts, and it seems like a waste of your time and talent. If I were a sales manager, I would take a look at everything my sales force had to do and immediately get rid of anything that got in the way of them actually being out there selling. I'd ask myself, *How much data collection can I farm out to a support staff? How much of it can I just get rid of altogether?* (By the way, this is just another way of saving intellectual and emotional energy, which you read about in Secret #16, Master the Day.)

For a performance review to be of value, you have to measure it against something. If you are a track-and-field high jumper, your performance is judged against a simple metric: Did you get over the bar?

Ah, if only it were that simple in sales.

"Setting the bar" for salespeople begins with the dreaded annual budget, in which the company establishes goals for them for the coming year. The process has its own unofficial time of year: budget season.

Sometimes the fun starts when a number is passed down

from on high. This holy number represents what the corporation expects in sales production. It usually goes to a sales manager, who fiddles with it, meets with his or her team, and asks, "Okay, everyone, here are the revenue projections for next year: How do you plan to make your numbers?" In another scenario, salespeople make their own projections based on their experience, their pipeline, and assorted other factors.

Why the obsession with all the measurements that track and (try to) predict sales? It's not complicated: Sales is the lifeblood of any business. It generates revenue, and without revenue . . . well, you know.

Measuring also temporarily allays fear. It provides proof that you're actually doing something. There are celebrations when you "make your numbers." There are bigger parties when you "exceed expectations." There are serious conversations when your numbers fall below their predictive goals. I get it. We all understand the necessity of measuring sales performance.

With all the metrics my interviewees already deal with, I was genuinely surprised to discover how many of them track *even more* things than they're required to. Yes, that sounds bizarre, but a lot of million-dollar salespeople do it, and to them it isn't at all a waste of time. Top producers don't measure their performances only by the required corporate yardsticks. They have their own personal metrics as well. The specific data top producers track and measure depends on their personalities and goals. Mary tracks the number of times she hears No for each sale. For example: Brandy, real estate agent extraordinaire from Secret #13, Not So Fast, keeps track of the clients who come to the fabulous parties she throws for past, present, and future customers every year. She knows who always shows up and who never does, and she uses her data to refocus some energy on the people who don't come. She knows that staying in touch with clients—even the ones from years ago—keeps her relationships strong. And strong relationships mean lots of referrals. So if she identifies certain clients who don't like parties, she knows to reach out to them in a different way.

But while Brandy's party metric is a hard number, other producers' personal metrics are pretty subjective and tougher to quantify. A lot of them keep tabs on intangible behaviors that they believe are instrumental to their success. It's also likely that nobody else cares about these personal metrics but the individual producers and their teams.

But producers will tell you that whatever it is they keep track of helps them understand their current positions and what they are building in the future.

Reggie has worked for the same company for fifteen years selling radiology equipment—the various medical machines that perform MRIs, CT scans, PET scans, ultrasounds, and X-rays. This equipment isn't cheap, but hospitals and clinics need it, and they have to buy it from someone.

Reggie is a brilliant producer who can talk knowledgeably about the impact of small-wave radiation versus magnetic fields with the best radiologists—or, for that matter, physicists—out there.

As a million-dollar saleswoman, Reggie, who's based in Chicago, keeps track of all the numbers her employer requires her to track. But she also follows a statistic that's *not* on her corporate scorecard: time spent selling. Yeah, how much of her workweek she actually spends doing her primary job, as opposed to non-revenue-generating activities like meetings and administrative duties.

JUST DO THE REPORT

Perhaps you feel the way Reggie does. "I spend way too much time filling out reports and not enough time selling," she told me. To get herself psyched up for the administrative chores, she reminds herself of the following:

This stuff is boring, but valuable. "My company tracks what they think is important," she says. "I like a lot of the metrics they use and understand their importance in the greater picture."

It's part of the job. "*I* work for *them*. There are requirements of being an employee, and one is to fill out the monthly reports. If I do what I am required to do, I am compensated for my efforts. It's an easy formula to understand."

It's less unpleasant to do it than not. "It's just too deflating to get 'called to the principal's office' when I'm late or short on their data." Use the information gleaned from your energy map (see Secret #16, Master the Day) to identify your own best time to tackle the reports.

Reggie collects her personal data privately, on her daily calendar. Whenever she has been engaged in a direct sales activity—whether that's a phone call, a client meeting, or a product presentation—she makes a note of how long she spent and logs an *s* in her datebook. So if she took an hour in the morning to answer client e-mails, she'll write in green ink, "9–10 a.m. = s." If she was out on sales calls in the afternoon, she'll write, "1–6 p.m. = s." All of this time, to her, is "Time Spent Selling."

What she is trying to determine is how much time does she need to spend in order to make a sale—and how much time during the day does she spend doing the parts of her job that frustrate her.

When Reggie invited me to look through her calendar, I opened it up to a random day and saw two *s* notations in green. "Bad day," she told me. "I only spent about two hours in what I think is actual selling." She pointed to an *m* on the same page, written in red ink. Ironically, she told me, when I asked her what the red *m* meant, "I was in a meeting most of the day reviewing new expense-tracking software. What a waste!"

Reggie's Time Spent Selling is a pretty subjective metric. It's up to her to decide what activities count as "selling," and to pay attention to how long she is engaged in those activities every day. But since she is the only person paying attention to her *s* markings, complete objectivity and accuracy aren't that important. What *is* important is that the metric helps inspire her and keep her focused. "Following my Time Spent Selling is important to me," she said. "I reset at the end of every day by looking at my green *s* tally." If there are a lot of *s* notations, she's happy. And if there aren't, "I know that tomorrow I'll have an opportunity to do better."

Another Chicagoan, Fitz, runs a very successful sales team from a gleaming tower on Wacker Drive, just off of Lake Michigan in the Windy City. Fitz has a challenge: Even though he is a sales powerhouse—"king of the seventeenth floor"—he often finds himself at odds with the behemoth global financial services corporation he works for. Fitz is one of just twenty-five U.S. (and seventy-five worldwide) sales managers. His job performance is affected by conditions well beyond his control, including corporate politics and the international economy. Fitz answers to the national director of sales, who sits in a New York office tower that looks out over the East River.

Years ago, Fitz discovered he had very little say in the metrics his company required of him. He thought there were some better measurements that would be more helpful and effective, and he pitched these ideas to his higher-ups. He didn't get far.

This put Fitz in a pickle, stuck between his employer's way and his own preferred way of measuring his performance. Eventually, though, he hit upon the idea to just go ahead and use his own metrics. He still complies with his company's requirements, of course, but he also measures his and his team's performance with his own special system. It goes like this:

First, define your objectives. Fitz and his team start this process by setting measurable goals, whether for the quarter, the year, or some other time frame. Ideally there are no more than three. They might be: (1) increase overall sales by X percent; (2) increase new accounts by Y percent; and (3) increase sales in a particular category by Z percent.

Next, focus on the actions that will cause the effect you're looking for. In their obsession with measurements and data, companies fixate on results, rarely studying what led to the results. Fitz understands that the best way to achieve a result is to know what causes it and do more of that. Because Fitz has been studying his team's technique for years, he likely already knows what it takes to, for example, land new customers. If his salespeople usually have to contact twenty new leads before they get interest, and he wants to add twenty new accounts over the next quarter, he'll instruct them to ramp up by calling four hundred prospects.

Fitz also is pretty aware of how he, as manager, can best help his sales force, whether that is accompanying people on sales calls or helping with presentations.

Finally, validate the results. After each sale, Fitz reviews the process from start to finish. In a short meeting with the team that closed the deal, Fitz will ask, "What do you think got you the result you were looking for?" Was it contacting four hundred people? Was it something else? He reviews his own involvement: Did he provide enough assistance? Was he too hands-on? Where did his help make a difference? He consolidates this information into a page of notes that will help him when he develops future action plans.

Fitz conducts a review of his goals and positions every day. The very first thing he does each morning is get on the company intranet and look at all the deals that went down the previous day. How did the other sales forces do? Is he ahead of them or behind them? If he's ahead, that bit of data validates his own actions. If those actions aren't paying off, he'll make an adjustment.

Fitz is a great example of a producer who does not passively await the corporate data dump. He and other salespeople in his league set their own internal goals, relying on their own metrics to help them succeed. Fitz's personal vision doesn't replace or compete with the corporate data. It just adds to his success. He compares his method versus his company's corporate method to a bowl of gumbo: a delicious mix of ingredients that work together to make something even better—in his case, an astounding sales record.

"Do you know why most people get out of bed every day?" Meredith asked me. We were sitting in her office. It was *very* small. There was room for her desk, a credenza, two tightly grouped chairs, and that was it.

"No, why?" I asked.

Meredith replied, "Neither do they."

I love that quote, because I think it's pretty true. However, it is not the case for Meredith. She gets out of bed every day because, to paraphrase *The Blues Brothers*, she is on a sales mission from God. Meredith sells millions of dollars' worth of homes in Dallas and is a big player in the city's real estate world. She also has her own dedicated assistant, which just shows how skilled she is at making deals. Most of the other agents in her office share a support staff. But a couple of years back, Meredith went to her office manager and put a contract on her desk. The contract said, essentially, *Give me a full-time support person and I will increase my sales by 15 percent in six months. If I don't, you can take my person back. Oh, and I want Janet.* She then signed the document in front of the office manager. Great drama—and so effective. She got Janet, and her sales went up by 19 percent!

Janet figures very prominently in Meredith's personal metric. She also ensures that every single one of Meredith's days starts exactly the same way. It's like the real estate version of *Groundhog Day*, except that instead of a clock radio jarring Bill Murray awake with yet another round of "I Got You Babe," Janet gets Meredith rolling by walking into her office with three information sets, against which Meredith will measure her performance for the day:

○ *Current client data.* This set of information involves buyers who have just settled on a house, buyers to whom Meredith is still showing houses, and sellers whose listings she is handling. How many clients are in each category? Do any need immediate attention?

○ *Prospective client data.* This is about filling the legendary sales pipeline. How many leads does Meredith have in the works? How many referrals does she need to follow up on?

○ *Action items.* This is the miscellaneous stuff Meredith needs to accomplish. Say Meredith and Janet are hosting a cocktail party at a house a client has listed. Some of the day's action items might have to do with that event. This data set might sound suspiciously like a to-do list, but remember, it's still a yardstick against which Meredith can measure her progress. With every item she crosses off, she is moving forward. It's a quantifiable measurement.

I especially like this routine because of the very visual way Janet presents Meredith with the data: on index cards in three different colors. Green index cards are for existing clients. Yellow cards are for prospective clients. White cards are action items.

Since the index cards are updated daily, the data on them stays current. And Meredith keeps those cards visible on the right side of her desk, a very tangible reminder of the data she is tracking that day.

Meredith's performance measurement system is highly personal. She uses these metrics to reset herself each morning and shape the day's actions based on what needs to be done. Her index cards create a strategy around activity. She works with purpose, based on the individualized performance metric she has developed over the years of her sales career. She measures what works for her.

Great salespeople develop very personal measurement models. They create key performance indicators that go beyond their corporate system. Their models help them reach aggressive goals and often contain "soft" data that can't be quantified in traditional ways. What metrics might work for you?

SECRET #18

Don't Waste Good

Every idea seems to have two potential outcomes. One of those outcomes is failure.

We spend a lot of time worrying about failure and how to correct it (see Secret #14, Embrace the Dark Side). We are taught early that the key to greatness is to improve at the skills we're bad at. Study harder to bring that D up to an A. Spend lots of time working with the weakest member of the team. And, of course, learn from every mistake. I have often heard consultants and leaders paraphrase the late Thomas J. Watson, the chairman and CEO of IBM from 1914 to 1956, who said that, in order to win, you need to double your rate of failure.

But with all of this focus on failure, we often forget the other side: Success!

In this book I have talked about failure as the first filter that culls the field of salespeople. To quote Mary, the insurance sales veteran you've already met a few times, who explained the importance of being the last one standing: "If you can't stomach a lot of doors slamming in your face, then you won't last long in this business."

Now it's time to look at the positive: Million-dollar producers take advantage of their accomplishments and mine success from success. They use their successes to become more successful. **They don't ignore their failures, but they also never brush aside what they do well.** They "Don't Waste Good."

Don't Waste Good is about looking at each sales transaction to figure out which specific actions you took paid off so you can replicate those things next time. The military uses a form of Don't Waste Good called an after-action review, a formal evaluation by participants and leaders of a project or exercise to analyze how events transpired, and why, and whether improvements could be made. In Don't Waste Good, though, the focus of this strategic analysis is on the positive. What went right?

When I formally began my study, I got to sit in on the million-dollar producer version of an after-action review at a property insurance wholesaler in Atlanta. In a small conference room, two superstar brokers and their administrative team sat down with their boss, who was an ex-military guy, and a pair of account managers, whose job it was to make sure all the post-sale paperwork was completed with *i*'s dotted and *t*'s crossed. The brokers and admins were required to answer a set of questions. These questions were the same for every post-sale debrief:

Identify the actions, in order, that resulted in the sale. The team re-created the deal step by step.

What worked? The team considered whether any particular actions were home runs in scoring the sale. They also noted any smaller actions that had also helped.

Why do you think it worked? The team members used past experience to answer this question.

Can we duplicate it again? If it was a one-off, that was fine. But one of the goals of this exercise was to identify elements of the process that could be replicated.

When the meeting was over, the boss sent a report to corporate headquarters to be disseminated to all thirty-five sales offices nationwide via an area of their corporate intranet titled "Sales Successes."

I asked Nick, one of the two brokers, "Is there a 'Sales Failures' section?"

He laughed. "Nope," he said. "That would fill our entire intranet."

During my study, I discovered that once great salespeople learn from their failures, they begin the equally crucial process of learning from their successes. They not only review every sale but they also ask themselves all-encompassing questions like "What do I do well?" and "How can I build on my positive qualities to improve my career?" They focus on their strengths instead of dwelling on their weaknesses. They plan for success. They approach it strategically.

A SUCCESS STORY

What could you accomplish if you focused on your strengths instead of obsessing over your weaknesses? Here's a little woodland fable to illustrate what I mean:

Deep in the forest, there is a small school with three students, a rabbit, a bird, and a fish. The teacher has three lessons to help them choose their future careers.

The first day's lesson is running. The instructor asks the rabbit to go first. The rabbit sprints left and right. He demonstrates a quick direction change and then slides to a stop right in front of the teacher, who says, "You are an outstanding runner!" Next up is the bird. The bird ponders the assignment and comes up with a plan: Though he can't run, he performs a series of quick little hops to mimic running. The teacher says to the bird, "You're a pretty good runner." Now it's the fish's turn. He has no legs; therefore, running is not an option, and so he does nothing. The teacher says, "Fish, you are a horrible runner."

That night the rabbit goes home thinking, *I'm a success!* The bird thinks, *I'm okay at this.* The fish thinks, *I am a failure.*

The next day's lesson is flying. Again the rabbit goes first. He knows he doesn't have the body for flight, but when he really tries, he can jump pretty far. He stands on a rock, leaps, and lands. The teacher says, "Rabbit, you're a pretty good flier." Next is the bird. Oh, the bird's heart swells. He knows: *This is my time.* He rises up, beats his wings, and performs barrel rolls, dead stalls, and, just for good measure, some loop-the-loops. The teacher exclaims, "You are an outstanding flier!"

Lastly it is the fish's turn. He looks up from his pond and simply shakes his head no. The teacher says, "You are a horrible flier."

By day's end, the rabbit still feels okay, although not quite as much as he did the previous day. The bird feels like a rock star. The fish, fins drooping, thinks he's the world's biggest loser.

The final lesson is swimming. The rabbit looks into the pond and thinks, *No way.* He sits on a rock for the remainder of the lesson. The bird longs for the webbed feet of a duck. Lacking that advantage, he perches on a branch. The fish can hardly contain his enthusiasm. *If it's swimming you want,* he thinks, *it is swimming you will get!* He does the backstroke, the breaststroke, the butterfly, and a few freestyle laps around the pond. He isn't even breathing hard. The teacher proclaims: "Fish, you are an outstanding swimmer! Rabbit and bird, you are both terrible swimmers."

At the end of the three lessons, the rabbit, the bird, and the fish decide the following: The rabbit will be in the running business. The bird will pursue a career in flying. The fish will start a swimming enterprise.

The moral: The best way to be successful is to do what you're good at. Learn how to manage your weaknesses. Take advantage of your strengths and build on them.

"We are at war," Susan told me, "*war.* We are fighting every single moment for market share, customers, and that top-of-mind place for our products in every client's thoughts."

Susan runs a team of pharmaceutical salespeople—"pill-and-juice pushers," as she jokingly calls herself and her group. (Yes, the joke is slightly dark, but that kind of humor is a part of life in pharmaceutical sales.) Susan's team is spread among three different cities in Texas, a huge territory that's "big enough to fill my worry cup," Susan told me.

We met in one of the conference rooms in Susan's Dallas office. At the head of the table was a map of Texas studded with red, yellow, and green pins. Each pin represented the location of a sales opportunity.

The yellow pins, Susan said, were future meetings: They had been set up but hadn't yet happened. The red pins represented meetings that hadn't resulted in a sale for whatever reason; whether because of timing, product positioning, or some other factor, the deal had gone wrong. But the green pins represented sales successes. "They show us where our process worked," Susan explained.

It is those green pins that Susan focuses on. You could call Susan's map the optimistic version of Roger's Wall in Secret #14, Embrace the Dark Side. Susan's strategy is to build on success, and she is an expert at figuring out what went *right*. To do this, Susan uses a continuous-feedback system that, like Nick's company's military-style debriefs, might come across as more than a little micromanaging.

After every sales call, Susan schedules a one-on-one debrief with the salesperson to discuss how it went, with an emphasis on "What did you do well?" Susan is in constant assessment mode. Piece by piece she takes apart the actions of her team member, looking for little things that worked and might improve the whole team's performance. This is far beyond what most managers do after a sales call. Susan doesn't just pop her head into a returning salesperson's office to ask, "How did it go?" Instead, she'll ask about the interaction between the salesperson and the customer. She'll ask how their company's other departments performed behind the scenes. Were the necessary marketing materials, like brochures and samples, available? Did the paperwork get done on time? (There are a lot of regulations associated with selling pharmaceuticals.) Although Susan inevitably hears about mistakes and missteps—the bad stuff—she is searching for what worked. Success is made up of a lot of ingredients, and Susan doesn't want to miss any of them. She Doesn't Waste Good.

After she gathers her data, Susan studies it. What can she repeat? How can this sales victory translate to the next sales victory? Can she come up with a model that can be replicated by salespeople with varied skills and personality types?

Susan has a firm understanding of her team's failures. But she has discovered that it is much easier to meet her sales goals by focusing on their achievements. She is looking to use what went right to make every future pin green.

It's true; sales folks are notorious complainers when they have to do any activity that does not have to do with selling— like attending this kind of meeting. And Susan's technique is time-consuming and meticulous. But Susan's people sure don't miss a debriefing session. While the strategy is intrusive at times, they recognize its value and believe in the results. Susan and her team lead their company in sales. So there's minimal grumbling.

Susan also knows something many aspiring winners don't recognize: Her team, like the rest of us, responds to reports of their successes better than they respond to reports of their failures. We constantly hear about "the wisdom of failure," but studies show that dwelling on what you did wrong can be a weak motivator compared to concentrating on what you do right.

Besides, everyone loves to celebrate what they're good at.

For example: Mary, the insurance superstar you're well acquainted with, always took a moment to commemorate every one of her hard-earned insurance sales. Mary had a brass captain's bell installed right next to the door outside her office. When she made a sale, she'd step into the hallway and give that old bell a couple of rings. It was loud and obnoxious. Her colleagues really hated that bell, but Mary's manager smiled every time he heard it.

"We call it 'KIST,'" Drew, another top producer in the insurance business, informed me.

"'KIST'?"

"Knowledge, instinct, skills, and tips. We look at everything through this lens. But, most importantly, we methodically examine our successes."

Drew is a consummate professional. I have never seen him wearing anything other than an elegant suit, crisp white shirt, spectacular tie and pocket square, and shoes that gleam. Drew once told me that he dresses this way even on days when he works from home. (I would swear he mows his lawn in a full suit and tie, if I thought Drew actually did his own yard work.) "How I feel dictates how I perform," he says. When I see him, he makes me feel underdressed in my jeans, sneakers, and aloha shirt, but Drew and I have worked together for years, and he lets me slide.

"KIST," an acronym I'd never heard before his interview, is a specific process Drew and his colleagues use to measure their success. The sales team analyzes its activities within each of the four categories using specific metrics so that everyone can learn within the same system. The sales meetings at Drew's New York office are called KIST meetings, and they are designed to identify the elements that make each sale successful so the team can leverage them in future sales.

USE LEVERAGE

People in business say "leverage" a lot to mean "make the best and most efficient use of." The idea is similar to the concept of leverage in physics.

Simply put, the law of the lever explains that if you use a fulcrum and a lever—a simple contraption that looks like a playground seesaw—you can lift very heavy objects relatively easily. (This law was proven by Archimedes, an ancient Greek whom you could describe as a Renaissance man, except that he lived thousands of years before the Renaissance. He was a physicist, mathematician, inventor, engineer, and astronomer. The guy could do it all.)

The nature of leverage is that the more of it you have, the less effort you must expend to get the job done. Minimum effort, maximum return.

In business, nothing is easier to leverage than success. It doesn't take much effort to do what you're good at. Once you identify your talents, you've done most of the heavy lifting.

Drew explained how KIST works:

- *Knowledge.* After every successful sale, the team seeks to answer two questions: First, "What did we need to know going into the sale?" and second, "What did we learn?" For example, the team reviews the contacts who helped get the sale rolling and determines whether there might be additional opportunities in those contacts.

- *Instinct.* A successful transaction is often made up of small nuances that move a "potential" sale into a "closed" sale. Team members try to identify and quantify the nebulous, intuitive qualities they brought to each deal. These are superstars who, through experience, have developed a kind of sales sixth sense. It's hard to define, but during the KIST process they talk about what they noticed during the process. During a conversation with a potential client, for example, one of Drew's salespeople sensed that the client was anxious and needed reassurance. A less experienced salesperson might have offered the client a list of references to call. But this salesperson whipped out his cell phone right there at the sales meeting, called an existing satisfied customer, and handed the phone to the nervous potential client.

- *Skills.* After every sale, the team wants to know what talents the producer brought to the transaction. Was it active listening? (See Secret #8, W.A.I.T.) Was it interpersonal communication? A killer presentation? If a specific skill led to a sale, is it worth starting a company-wide training program to strengthen that skill in everyone?

○ *Tips.* The team asks, "What simple suggestions from this experience can you share?" The salesperson might say, "I noticed that the client had tons of family pictures around his office, and when I asked him about them, he went on and on. He loved talking about his family, and it created a very open feeling to the meeting." The tip: Pay attention to your surroundings during a sales call.

By focusing on what they are good at, Susan and Drew aren't just cockeyed optimists. They systematically study their talents and how those talents help close deals. They think about how to replicate their successes in the future.

The bottom line is that success is great raw material for improvement and deserves a place in your sales process. Success *can* be defined. And when you take time to identify what you do right, it becomes everyone's strength.

SECRET #19

Bang Your Drum

In sales, you are the CEO of yourself. You are the chief strategy officer of your sales process. You are the head of marketing, and you'd better be marketing *you*. Since sales is about relationships, and relationships are solidified when your clients clearly understand the particular value you bring to their lives, it makes sense for a salesperson to create his or her own idea of a brand. In fact, million-dollar producers spend as much energy differentiating themselves from other salespeople as their companies expend on differentiating their corporate brand from other companies.

This isn't a particularly new idea. The problem is, after a pretty good run of self-branding hot talk a couple of decades ago, the idea that you are as powerful a brand as your company is has taken a backseat to newer ideas, both on the corporate level and, more important, on the individual level.

Except in the case of million-dollar salespeople. Secret #19 acknowledges: **If you want to get to the top of the heap, you must think of yourself as a brand, and you absolutely must market yourself as such. Clearly, enthusiastically, and constantly.**

THE TRENDY TRAP

The sales world is constantly searching for the next Big Idea—the ultimate indispensable action item or must-do management theory. But business's notoriously short attention span and lack of commitment mean most of these notions have about as much staying power as predawn mist. Just as you realize it's there, it's already dissipating.

This is true of the self-branding strategy, which was a Big Idea in business in the late 1990s and has now become sort of ho-hum and expected; everyone—or at least everyone under the age of thirty-five—has played around at creating their own online identity via social media. Even though it's not the trendiest Big Idea anymore, the strategy still makes a lot of sense, especially in sales. Everyone has a chance to be unique, to stand out, and a commitment to doing so is an avenue to success.

The first step to mastering Bang Your Drum is recognizing and celebrating your own uniqueness. T.C., the financial services wholesaler from Secret #11, Charm the Gatekeepers, didn't set out to develop a personal brand around regularly having pizza delivered to his clients' offices. You could even argue that the whole association between T.C. and pizza is at odds with his persona and product. After all, T.C. wears a suit and tie every day, drives an impressive foreign sports car, and deals in sophisticated investments. But if his customers' support staffs remember him as the Pizza Guy, and if that title opens more doors for him, T.C. is happy to embrace it. It's his. He owns it.

As you're trying to figure out what makes you stand out from the crowd, it's important to understand the goal of developing a personal brand. It's actually very logical. The goal is: *How can I get my market to think of* me?

Clay, a very successful salesman at one of the largest car dealerships in Louisiana, made this discovery early on: He realized that the car company he worked for did a great job of getting buyers to think of its brand by identifying the features that made its vehicles special. Meanwhile, Clay's New Orleans dealership did pretty much everything it could to make it easy for its salespeople to move cars. "They made great financing available. They allowed us to sweeten a deal with extras, including free car washes and oil changes," he said.

But neither the manufacturer nor the dealership was in the business of helping Clay and his fellow salespeople build their own personal brands. And if you, too, work for a big corporation, chances are yours doesn't encourage you to stand out, either. Think about it: Why would it, really? The company's interest is selling its product or service. It makes no difference to the organization whether you do the selling or the salesperson in the office next to you does it.

It was among some of America's best examples of personal branding that I found myself interviewing Clay. New Orleans's French Quarter is full of talented street musicians who play on corners, in alleys, and around the magnificent Jackson Square. Each vies for your attention, hoping some of your spare change ends up in his or her open guitar case. These artists are brilliant self-marketers who work hard to differentiate themselves from their competitors through the instruments they play or by putting their own spin on crowd-pleasing popular songs.

It was among these competing musicians that I found myself interviewing Clay, after I was able to convince him to endure the parking nightmare of the French Quarter and meet me at Café Du Monde for café au lait and beignets, one of his city's greatest treats.

Clay doesn't specialize in fancy foreign cars but in a great American brand. His vehicles don't pull in $100,000 each; Clay needs to sell a lot of them to be the top producer. And sell a lot he does.

One big secret to Clay's success is that he is a self-branding dynamo. Even first-time customers often know him by name when they walk in. This is particularly impressive when you consider that your average first-time auto buyer rarely knows, let alone cares, who sells them their new wheels. "People come to the dealership in search of a car, not in search of a salesperson," Clay told me.

After realizing this, Clay faced a challenge. It wasn't just how to get buyers to come into the dealership. It was *How do I get them to come in and ask for* me? he explained. "I needed them to think of Clay, and I needed them to do it way before they got to the showroom."

Clay thought long and hard about how to differentiate himself. He studied the problem. He sought out successful salespeople each with his or her own individual identity. Finally, Clay lit on an idea. He launched his own YouTube channel and started making videos. Every week Clay shoots a simple five-minute video in which he answers questions about buying cars. He uses his years of experience to advise viewers about the process, especially the top issue on any car buyer's mind: How can I get the most car for the least money?

These videos are simple and inexpensive to shoot, and Clay is a funny and personable star (which you'd kind of expect from a car salesman). Clay also writes a very cool blog about trends, features, and all manner of car stuff, and embeds his videos in the blog, too. Through all of this, Clay never pushes his brand or his dealership. He just focuses on providing expert guidance to anyone looking for a car. "I can become people's source for information. Not high-pressure sales, but information," he said.

You might think Clay's dealership, or at least the national brand's compliance department, would want a say in his videos. I was curious about how much control Clay's employers exerted over his content. What did they tell him when he first asked their permission to start posting videos?

Clay explained that he didn't ask. He just started doing it. It never occurred to him to seek his company's approval first— although his wry smile suggested he might be an "Ask for forgiveness, not permission" kind of person. Since he started doing the videos, Clay went on, he'd had a number of meetings with management and the national folks, but not so they could scold him. Instead, they wanted Clay to teach others how to develop similar strategies that get to the "Think of me" end goal. Has he ruffled a few feathers along the way? Sure. But I can say with assurance that just about every big-time salesperson I interviewed has been in the doghouse with management at one time or another.

Over a second batch of beignets, Clay pulled out his iPad and showed me some videos and blog postings. He smiled, a little powdered sugar on his lips, and said, "Bingo. People come in and ask for Clay!"

THE PATTON BRAND

There's no better example of a self-branding genius than General George S. "Old Blood and Guts" Patton, the World War II tank commander who was instrumental in defeating Nazi Germany.

Patton recognized that by playing up his success, courage, and bravado before a military foray, he could intimidate the enemy ahead of time, giving him an edge in the eventual battle. He deliberately crafted a tough-talking, aggressive public persona, even practicing his trademark scowl, which he called his "war face," in the mirror. He leveraged this persona to become a true force of fear. (It also helped that he had the chops to back up his swagger.) Patton understood the concept of *How can I get the enemy to* think of me *before I even arrive at the battlefield?*

Believe it or not, Patton's and Clay's strategies both spring from a similar setup. Think about it: The U.S. Army gave Patton most of what he needed to succeed, including supplies, equipment, ammunition, and troops. Patton supplied his own personal brand to close the deal.

There's more to you than just your job description. You know you have something special to offer, and it's up to you not only to figure out what that special something is but also to make sure everyone knows it. Your company won't do this for you. No one but you will do this for you, and unless you want to remain an average producer, you'll consider self-promotion an unpaid part of your job that will provide a real return over the long term.

Nelson, who represents tenants looking for office space in Los Angeles, is known as the guy who cares about his clients beyond their leases. Nelson knows everything about his key clients. I mean *everything*. He knows where they went to college. He knows their hobbies. He knows what they like to read. He knows their favorite restaurants. He knows the names of their children and their extracurricular activities. It might sound kind of creepy, but it's really not; Nelson has acquired this knowledge over the long haul, and he uses it to build his personal brand.

Nelson specializes in technology companies, the type of firms that grow and need more space. And if you need more space and Nelson has done his job, you call him again. Oh, by the way, Nelson is one of the top commercial brokers in town. So how does he leverage his personal brand to make sure his clients keep him in mind the next time they double in size and need more room—and don't just go with whatever other top broker happens to contact them at the right time? Here are just two of many examples:

The cardinal and the gold. One of Nelson's clients was a University of Southern California alum, which Nelson of course knew. When the USC Trojans announced the selection of a new football coach, Nelson arranged for his client to go to a private meet and greet for the coach.

News they can use. Nelson's company puts out a monthly e-mail newsletter, kind of a State of the Union address for local commercial real estate with news about who leased what space, new space becoming available, and commercial buildings under construction. Nelson customizes part of the newsletter for his clients by adding a section called "Did You Know?" This is a place for news that has nothing to do with office space but *is* geared toward his key clients' interests. If he has a client who loves Italian food, Nelson might share news of a new Italian eatery opening up near that client's place of business. If the client is a movie nut, he might link to previews of upcoming blockbusters. If you're one of Nelson's clients and are into sailing, you just might find the latest on the America's Cup. With just a little research on top of his knowledge of his clients, Nelson uses his newsletter and his special perks to create a unique personal brand: the commercial real estate broker who personally cares about the people he does business with.

So what do you need to do to bring Secret #19 into your sales arsenal? Try these three tips to build your own personal brand:

- *Enhance your profile.* Clients love doing business with salespeople known as experts in their field. How do you get to be an expert? Study up. (See Secret #9, Sell Smart.) How do you get to be *known* as an expert? Through strategic exposure. Volunteer to teach and speak at industry events. Sit on panels at meetings and conferences. Write for trade publications. Post your industry-related thoughts on your blog. Take classes that add professional designations. As you build your reputation as a well-educated person, you simultaneously build your personal brand as a knowledgeable sales pro.

o *Demonstrate your unique value.* Your clients already know you understand whatever it is you sell; they would expect nothing less from you. So what can you do to demonstrate value in a surprising way, like T.C., Clay, and Nelson? Consider a newsletter, social media, or special events that demonstrate your own special contribution to your clients' lives. *Don't be shy.* You have to be aggressive in letting the world know how great you are. I am amazed at how many salespeople don't do this. Yes, shouting your successes from the rooftop can be obnoxious, but you can do it much more subtly. Here's a simple example: When you attend an industry event at which you have the opportunity to hear others share their knowledge, you should let your clients know. Pick your top five or ten accounts and send each one a handwritten note. It could read something like "I recently had the opportunity to participate in [my industry]'s annual leadership conference. I met with experts X and Y and heard some compelling new ideas. I would welcome the opportunity to meet with you and share how these ideas can create positive impact for you. I'll call next week to discuss a meeting time that works for you." How many of those clients will take your call?

Just about every one. The more visible you are, the more visible you become, because visibility has a way of increasing and multiplying. So spread the word!

END UP IN THE "SAVE" STACK

Everyone occasionally gets the Valpak in the mail. This is the envelope filled with discount coupons for a wide variety of local businesses. If the Valpak makes it into your house and you open it, I'm betting you play the "value game": You tear open the envelope, start to go through the various killer deals, and create two piles of coupons: the no pile and the yes pile. My personal internal monologue goes like this: *Hmm, let's see . . . nope, don't need teeth whitening, gutter repair, a new garage door, pest control, or landscaping,* I think, putting those coupons into the no pile. *But . . . hey! Two-for-one burgers at our favorite diner? Yes. Buy-one-get-one-free pizza, yes. Shirts laundered for 59 cents at the dry cleaner we already use? Yes!*

In a matter of moments you determine what is and is not of value to you. You might not have gone to that pizza joint without the two-for-one coupon. But that deal has now put this particular spot at the top of your pizza mind!

Your clients and prospects are playing the same game. What pile do you want to be in? Bang your drum, shout out your unique skills to your clients, and you'll end up in their "save" stack.

So don't be shy. Don't be average. And don't expect for one minute that anyone back at your office will call your clients and say, "Hey, Marge, Rafaela is doing great work for you. Thought you'd like to know." Positioning yourself at the top of your clients' minds is *your* job. In fact, it turns out, it's a critical part of your job. It can provide the separation and differentiation you desperately need in a highly competitive market. And it will help get you to the million-dollar level.

SECRET #20

You Can't Fake Real

"You're the real deal." Emily, a financial services advisor, can remember the exact moment when a potential client told her that. It was after the second of a pair of meetings Emily had carefully pursued with a wealthy investor she hoped to add to her book of business.

What did Emily's desired client mean by "the real deal"? He meant that he found her authentic and genuine, relaxed and sincere. Nothing rang untrue about the way she did business or the kind of person she was, and that appealed to him.

At this compliment, I doubt Emily did anything more than say thank you. But in her imagination I'm guessing she was punching the air like Rocky on the steps in Philadelphia. Imagine you had just impressed a prospect who could, with a simple "Let's do it," make your whole sales year. Just one deal with this guy would lift the revenue production weight off your shoulders, bringing in enough money that the rest of your year would be pressure-free. That would be a significant deal, a really important meeting. And, by the way, he did say, "Let's do it," gave her a huge piece of business, and is now one of her biggest clients.

Emily is at the very top of her game. She works with the upper echelon of investors (the big fish from Secret #12, Save the Whales). To get to these people, you need a wide breadth of skills, knowledge, and experience, and you also need a certain kind of steady self-confidence. Not one of these captains of industry would waste even a fraction of a second on a salesperson who was not "the real deal."

Emily was one interviewee in my study who instinctively followed almost every one of the 21 Secrets before I had even formally identified them. She is the master of her day, time-blocking her to-do list to stay organized. She is the queen of OLA. She obviously knows all about whales. Almost all her new clients are referrals from other clients; she mines success from success.

In addition to these winning sales behaviors, Emily shines with confidence and authenticity. Her secret is the basis of Secret #17: **The *realness* a million-dollar salesperson exudes is the result of careful preparation.**

During our interview, Emily told me about the very first meeting she had with the new client in the above example, the one who eventually got her to that second, face-to-face, real-deal handshake victory moment. She first learned of this investor from one of her clients, who shared that a friend was dissatisfied with his current investment team and was looking to expand his field of financial advisors. Emily politely asked if the client might introduce her to this friend. The minute that client said, "I'll see what I can do," Emily went into super-detective mode. That's right: She, like almost all million-dollar sales professionals, began to prepare for a meeting not yet even on her calendar.

"At this point," Emily told me, "I'm like a pilot on the landing approach. I am focused and attentive to the task at hand."

In a world in which a few keystrokes can open up someone's entire professional life, research is no longer an arduous task. (Emily has been in the business long enough to remember going to the city library on Indiana Jones–style treasure-hunting expeditions to unearth information.) These days, online fact-finding is so easy that any salesperson can quickly learn all the basics about a potential client, like exactly what he does for a living and at what company. But if you rely only on information you can get while sitting in front of a monitor, you will likely not be prepared at the level really important clients expect. To be authentic, you need to add a layer, and Emily does just that.

After she finds out all the basic stuff, Emily takes a deeper plunge and talks to her existing clients. She reviews and picks out any current clients who are likely to know the potential new client, maybe through work or through sitting on the same board of directors. She places a few calls and asks questions to help fill in the gaps. She will already know the new client's investment style. She'll know the charities he supports. She'll know his equity position in his company. In essence, she'll know all the decimal points. What she seeks are the personal elements that make him *who* he is, not *what* he is.

Clients are drawn to salespeople who are comfortable in their own skin, and Emily's advance preparation allows her to be this way. It is impossible, in fact, to be authentic when you're unprepared and scattered. "When I follow my process, I can relax, because preparation gives me comfort," she told me. "I have all the ammunition I need, so then I can do my thing."

For a look at how Emily's preparation helps her to be the real deal, here's how the first meeting went with that new client:

After a few e-mails and calls, the potential client agrees to give Emily some time on the phone. In that first phone call, he tells her, "You come highly recommended." BINGO! This magic phrase is an invitation for Emily to take a little risk and leverage some of her fact-finding.

She knows he's married, so she asks, "Can your wife attend the meeting, too?"

There's a pause. "You'd have to come out to the house."

"No problem," Emily says. "Let's find a time that works for all of us." (Note that she hasn't said "a time that works for you and your wife" but "a time that is also convenient for me." She wants to even the playing field by reminding the potential client that her time is valuable, too.)

Emily plans to create a relationship between not just her and the potential client but between her, him, and hopefully his entire family—because wealthy investors tend to have wealthy kids who also become investors.

After coffee at the couple's home, where Emily leads a conversation about everything from their college alma maters to classic philosophy (which the client had studied), Emily shakes hands and says she'll be in touch. She used her preparation to forge a personal connection, and it worked. After landing her second meeting, she positions her financial ideas and receives her first piece of business. That client is now one of Emily's largest and a steady source of referrals.

So let's talk about the hard-earned value of authenticity—of being the real deal, the real McCoy.

THE REAL MCCOY

I've always loved the phrase "the real McCoy." Although scholars aren't sure where it came from, these are two possibilities:

- In the 1870s, Elijah McCoy, a Canadian-American inventor, patented a lubrication system for locomotives that was so superior to other systems that railroad engineers would ask, "Is this engine equipped with the real McCoy system?"
- During Prohibition in the 1920s, independent rum smuggler Bill McCoy competed against organized crime by making his own product that was uncut and pure. People hankering for a drink at speakeasies would ask if the rum was "the real McCoy."

Which, if either, of these stories describes the true origin of "the real McCoy"? Who knows. But the lesson is a good one: Give people quality, "the real deal," and they will ask for you by name.

Theo sells real estate, and lots of it, on the East Coast. One of the things he said that stuck with me was that, despite his success, when a new acquaintance asks, "What do you do?" and Theo says he's in sales, he sometimes senses a hint of suspicion or wariness. "People think salespeople are just in it to get their commission, no matter what. People think we are in the business of deceiving them. We face this uphill battle from day one!"

Theo is able to change people's minds pretty quickly. But to be fair to those civilians who doubt salespeople's motives or honesty, every customer in America has at one time or another experienced some pretty inauthentic treatment. And phoniness is, unfortunately, baked into the sales culture. Corporate training begins the process of stripping away salespeople's individuality and indoctrinating them into "the way we do things." Salespeople are given scripts and expected to follow them to the letter. It's sales by rote, and it is terrible.

IS THIS YOUR FIRST TIME
HEARING US RECITE THESE LINES?

There is a particular Hilton I stay in very regularly when I travel to visit one of my favorite clients. I have checked into that hotel about half a dozen times a year for the past eight years. Yet, every time, the desk clerk, after asking to see my ID, scanning my credit card, entering my loyalty number, and giving me the once-over, will ask, "Is this the first time you've stayed with us?" Every time! One of the last times this happened, I said, "Do you realize that somewhere in Houston there is a guy using a laptop computer to drive a robotic vehicle on the planet Mars, yet your guest software system can't identify someone who has stayed at your hotel over fifty times? What if I tell you, 'Yes, it's my first time staying here'? What happens then? Do I get a tour of the hotel? Do I get a special parking space? Why do you ask me that every time?"

(Okay. After six hours of mind-numbing travel, I occasionally find it difficult to keep my sarcasm in check.)

"It's part of our welcome script," the clerk answered.

Sales by script. There you go.

In all fairness, the clerk probably doesn't even realize she is in sales. Still, she is the living, breathing spirit of the hotel and the first person guests come into contact with. Though her job description might not say "sales," she is a sales professional. (Remember when I said that in the introduction? Nearly everyone in the working world is selling something, whether they think they are or not.)

A script can be an important road map, but if sticking to it removes every shred of personal connection, the entire experience becomes annoyingly void of emotion. That is the opposite of authentic.

Theo's real estate conversations, on the other hand, are the opposite of scripted. They're relaxed and natural, "and take the tension out of the process," he says. "My customers even comment about how natural the whole process was when we send out surveys." The key to this ease? You guessed it. It's not memorizing dialogue. It's preparation. "Being prepared lets me be me, and clients can feel that. I become relatable," Theo observes.

Theo got into the million-dollar club by being in a constant state of study. He has been through so many market and industry changes that he has developed a chameleon-like ability to adapt to whatever is happening in his business.

"In the old days—which could mean yesterday—people relied on their real estate professional to do almost everything," he told me. "Before the Internet, agents were the only ones with access to the Multiple Listing Service, a database of all homes currently on the market. We didn't just show homes, either; we helped buyers get mortgages and insurance. These days, buyers can access all kinds of data. They've become overnight experts on everything from remodeling to negotiating to even flipping homes for magical profits." Now that real estate brokers and their agents are no longer the only source for home information, Theo said, "The reality is that we have to work smarter."

So Theo, like other producers in his category, focuses on making the home-buying or home-selling experience as pleasant as possible for his clients. He does this in part by studying up on any and all questions his Internet-schooled buyers might have for him.

"When we enter a neighborhood that has a home the buyer found online, I will not only know more about that home than they ever dreamed, I will know about the neighborhood and I'll probably know the neighbors," he told me. "I'll know how far away that home is from key highways, in both miles and driving time. I'll even know the best times to be on the road and when to stay home. They will ask questions, and I will have the right answers, because at the core of my job I am prepared."

THE TRUTH IS OUT THERE

A century ago, Winston Churchill said, "The truth is incontrovertible." You can't dispute it. In sales, truth is the foundation of authenticity. An authentic salesperson is true to him- or herself.

This is often a problem. A number of top producers I interviewed told me it took a while to find their sales "home"—a company that matched their style. To really be authentic, you need to find a sales culture that values authenticity and integrity.

Want to see the opposite of "the real deal"? Try to sell something you don't believe in. The charade is as clear as glass. At the gut level, your client will know something is wrong. But if you're really and truly engaged in your product or service, customers will see that you sell beyond commissions.

Top salesperson after top salesperson told me the same thing: Knowing your stuff gives you a sense of sales power, and it gives you the opportunity to be yourself so that you're not doing sales by rote but sales by *you*. When you come prepared to meetings and other sales situations, the pieces of your career start to fall together. You develop stronger relationships with your clients. You build an industry reputation. You are known as smart and reliable in a world where most of your competitors aren't. You create value at a personal level, a level beyond what you're selling.

If you know that it's not just your product or service that's important to your client, but that you yourself play a major role in the relationship—if you want to make a difference and are hungry for genuineness in your professional and personal life—then you already have much in common with million-dollar producers. Practice, prepare, and focus, and the real you will shine through.

SECRET #21

Become Your Product

Marcus is a car salesman. That is how he describes himself. He's proud of the title. He comes from a car family. An *American*-car family. His father worked on the Mustang line for Ford in Dearborn, Michigan. No one in his family has ever owned a foreign car.

Marcus was looking for a new salesperson to join his team at the Los Angeles dealership where he sells American muscle cars. He wanted a superstar with a lot of experience, someone already successful. He sent out feelers and tapped his network. He found a strong prospect and invited him to have coffee at the dealership. When the candidate drove up in a beautiful BMW, the interview was already over.

That's how important American cars are to Marcus's identity. Marcus, just like every one of the top producers I interviewed, *is* his product. There is no boundary between what Marcus sells and who he is.

The last secret of million-dollar salespeople is this complete identification with what they sell. Top producers enjoy a unique bond with their products or services and the companies they work for. It's a connection that increases over time, and, at its peak, it is hard to define where the salesperson ends and the product begins.

In the words of another top producer, Eli, "I see everything, every project, every idea, through the lens of this company. Its history, successes, failures, and breakthroughs are the essence of how I think. All I am is a result of my firm."

Eli works at an advertising agency and was a liberal arts major. But, he explained to me, he was kind of a science geek. (That was putting it mildly. This guy knew more about certain fields of science than I did, and I was a science student in college.) He used an interesting science analogy to explain his role at his firm.

"How much do you know about magnets?" Eli asked me. He went on to explain that magnets attract some metals and repel others. "Magnets grab ferrous metals—metals that contain iron—and hold on to them with a fierce grip. But they shrug their shoulders at other metals and leave them be."

Just as I was wondering what magnets had to do with sales, Eli said this: "We want to find the ferrous-metal clients, and I'm the magnet for our company."

Clients are attracted to salespeople who are as connected to and enthusiastic about what they sell—and for whom—as Eli is.

Eli is a smart guy, and at his agency, where he is a partner, he is a triple threat. His primary role is in sales: He presents campaign ideas to prospective clients. But he's also a key member of his agency's creative team, generating ideas for new campaigns. On top of that combination of responsibilities—already very unusual in the advertising world—Eli serves as an account manager, handling the campaigns once they're sold and serving as a go-between for his agency and the companies and brands it represents. Eli is not just *kind of* different—he is *really* different. His divergent skills make him one of his firm's most valuable assets.

Eli has been with his Chicago agency since it first opened its doors in 1980. He started as a graphic artist, but as the agency grew, he began doing a little bit of everything. Once he made partner, he told me, "I kind of fell into this multidiscipline job." Somewhere along the line, Eli's own personality merged with that of his company. He became the product.

The list of stories goes on and on. I met T.J., the in-house sales leader for a big home builder, where T.J. is the king of their custom division. He lives, breathes, and loves the homes he sells, which go for as much as $4 million.

"I spend a lot of my time going to look at other builders' work," he told me. "The homes look nice, but I notice things. We would never allow gaps at connection points for crown molding, for example. We are way better than that."

Just listening to T.J. talk, I could feel his connection to and pride in what he sold. It was palpable.

Developing this link between yourself and what you sell is crucial to career success. Think about it: Could a salesperson generate a million dollars' worth of sales of anything without a firm belief in the "anything" he or she is selling? In fact, forget about just *belief*; could a million-dollar producer do this without an emotional attachment to his or her product or service? Could he or she do it without *love*?

So where does this bond come from? A lot of it emerges through time and longevity. By the time you've made it to the million-dollar ranks, something has happened to you. During your career journey, you have not only honed your sales skills but also made a full commitment to what you do. That process starts at the place you work, so let's start our connective journey there.

I heard this all the time from my interviewees: "I love this company."

It wasn't "I like working here." It was "I *love* working here."

Before million-dollar salespeople achieve their status, they first must become part of a company that values their talents and lets them fly. The fact is, you can't become a superstar producer as part of a company you can't stand. You can't dread going to work and then turn around and hit milestone numbers. That just doesn't happen in sales. If you're back in a warehouse or a dark little cubicle and hate what you do and where you work, you might still be able to perform well enough to get by, but not if you want to be a sales superstar. To reach the million-dollar club, you can't keep your head down and hope nobody notices. There are simply too many human interactions in sales. You have to love what you do and the company you do it for. And if you don't, you probably have to find a place that you do love. It's important to note that many of the superstar producers in this study were on their second, third, or fourth company before they truly began to shine. It's up to you to find the right place for you.

The organization you work for must have a culture that supports its sales department. This means sales is not isolated from all the other company functions. A highly successful company won't just have a "sales-supportive" culture; it will have a "sales-friendly" culture. It will steadfastly see your department as not just a means to an end but as a partner in its success. That overall corporate view of sales is fundamental to a salesperson seeing the company's product or service as an extension of him- or herself.

If the sales department is consulted in the marketing of a product or service, the salesperson will feel that he or she is a key link between the company and its customers.

Imagine the opposite: a company in which marketing operates in its own silo and then gives the sales department all the stuff—supporting documents, brochures, promotional souvenirs, whatever—that marketing believes is needed to sell whatever is being sold. The salespeople receive all of this stuff and think, *What is this? This isn't what our clients want. What am I supposed to do with this?* During one of my interviews, a superstar producer kept having to move his chair to avoid an open cardboard box on the floor near his desk. He finally said to me, annoyed, "You know what's in the box? Logo coffee mugs from marketing. They want me to leave behind a mug every time I meet with a client. Why would I do that? My clients don't want another coffee mug. We get stuff like this all the time—stuff we never use. You could fill up a room with it."

He stopped to take a breath. Then he asked me, "Do you want a mug?"

I declined.

But when sales is involved from the get-go, they can advise marketing, bringing insights from their experience with clients. When this happens, the salesperson starts to connect to the product.

This is what is meant by a sales *culture*. Companies that cultivate million-dollar producers do so with a sales-friendly environment. They involve sales in decisions, in planning, and in budgeting. Sales becomes an element in their success. Without this corporate attitude, it's nearly impossible to create a sales force that will yield big-time production.

THE TIDIEST PLACE ON EARTH

If you are ever called to a corporate campus for a job interview, pay attention to the trash.

I once had dinner with a top executive at Disney. Over the meal, the executive told me a remarkable hiring story. He had been looking for a new, top-level employee and had narrowed the field down to two candidates. Each candidate was asked to come in for a face-to-face interview.

Before each interview, my client told me, he put an obviously empty soda can on the pathway into the building where the meeting was to be held. Then he watched the candidate approach the building. He waited. He wanted to see if either candidate would pick up the can and throw it away. He told me he couldn't imagine hiring someone who would pass by a piece of trash at Disney. "If you love something," the executive told me, "you take care of it." He wanted to see how connected each candidate was to the company he so identified with.

Guess what? Each candidate picked up the soda can and threw it out, leaving my executive friend with two excellent potential choices.

The next step to Become Your Product or service is insatiable curiosity. That's a quality you bring to the table.

"You could fill a library with what I know about this stuff." I heard variations on this statement all the time. Great salespeople spend copious amounts of time learning, often incidentally, about their fields. You can't be in love with something you don't really know. This fascination goes beyond the activities you enjoy in your off-hours, like movies or music. (We Jimmy Buffett fans know all the words to all of Buffett's songs. His concerts are twenty-thousand-person sing-alongs.) It permeates your work. If you are a million-dollar car salesman like Marcus, or like Sonny from Essential Secret #1, SIMPLE, or Jeff from Secret #6, Build Your "Like" Platform, I guarantee you know how an engine works and can identify almost any vehicle model and year as it speeds past you on the highway. Million-dollar property and casualty insurance salespeople chitchat with underwriters about risk. Life insurance salespeople hang out with actuaries and know their way around a life-expectancy chart.

The superstars who sell complex robotic surgical equipment, like Billy from Essential Secret #4, Make Friends First, spend time with the engineers and doctors who designed the machines. Pharmaceutical superstars hang out with chemists. I know a grocery chain that sends all its produce clerks to the local farms that supply the chain's tomatoes and lettuce. The produce clerks have more expertise than some of the sales folks I work with!

This commitment becomes a binding element to all of their relationships—not just between the salesperson and the client, but between the salesperson and the company. Great producers develop a sense of duty to these relationships.

There were many times in my interviews when an interviewee was talking and talking and raving about what they sold, and I'd find my mind wandering. I'd be starving and thinking about soup. These people are *so attached* to what they sell. But unless you're really desperate for lunch, this is a good thing. Million-dollar sales professionals really believe in their products and services.

MR. DR PEPPER

Years ago, I was playing in a foursome at a corporate golf tournament in Texas. Another player at the tournament was W. W. "Foots" Clements, the legendary executive responsible for a huge hunk of the success of my favorite soft drink, Dr Pepper.

The late Mr. Clements was an unbelievable Horatio Alger story. He started as a Dr Pepper delivery boy and rose to be chairman and CEO of his company. If you'd pierced this guy's veins, I swear he would have bled Dr Pepper.

So when a beverage cart attendant stopped at the fourth hole to ask if any of the golfers wanted anything, Foots furrowed his brow. The only soft drinks on the cart were those of a competitor. Foots, a consummate Texas gentleman who wore cowboy boots and string ties, didn't get mad. He motioned to the young woman. "Here's some money," he said. "Please get rid of all the drinks on your cart, and any other cart on this golf course, and replace them with the following." He then wrote down a list of all his company's products on a scorecard and gave it to the attendant, along with a nice-size tip.

Lo and behold, less than an hour later, the drink cart returned, and now only Dr Pepper products graced its ice-filled chests. It was unthinkable for Foots to drink anything other than the product he represented. His commitment to Dr Pepper was all-encompassing.

For my very last example of this phenomenon, meet Kei, the top—and possibly only—salesman at a bakery in the South that makes fried pies. These are the tasty packaged impulse buys you usually find by the cash register at convenience stores, though Kei is working hard to see to it that his company's pies end up everywhere in America. That includes movie theaters, auto parts stores, hardware chains, and any other place whose customers might want a little treat.

Kei is a big fish in a very small pond and kind of snuck into my study. He doesn't fit into any of the seven chosen industries, which makes him a million-dollar outlier. But make no mistake: He is a major sales professional.

I spent a long time over a long dinner listening to Kei talk about crunchy crust and creamy filling. He was passionate about the quality of his company's pies. He was passionate about the variety: He sells over twenty flavors, including chocolate, apple, lemon, and blueberry. And Kei uses his passion to deliver delicious profits.

Kei told me about how he got his product into a big supermarket chain. Now, in the supermarket world, getting a new product into stores is like trying to penetrate a fortress. And when you are a small company that sells only one little product, it's like trying to pierce that wall with a toothpick. But to Kei it is inconceivable that everyone wouldn't want to carry his pies. So after going through all the traditional hoops to try to get an audience with the supermarket chain's buyer, Kei went Niagara Falls on them. He sent some pies to the supermarket chain's corporate office.

Wait—did I say *some*? I mean, he sent *hundreds* of pies in every flavor. Boxes and boxes of pies arrived at the buyer's office. The buyer tried a few and, as Kei predicted, fell in love with them and started to hand them out to everyone at the company. Clerks and secretaries asked, "Can I have some pies to take home?" "Are there any more of the lemon ones?" "We are going to carry these, right?"

Abracadabra. Like magic, Kei landed shelf space for his pies.

Kei is his product. His product is Kei.

After our dinner, Kei reached into his backpack and gave me a pie. "I don't have business cards," he said. "I have these."

It was delicious.

*　　*　　*

People see the sales culture depicted in movies as soul-robbing and deadening. They think of boiler rooms full of salespeople condemned by quotas and arbitrary deadlines. But the great producers I spoke with see and feel the opposite. They are committed to a profession they love. They are connected to a product they believe in. They are part of their organization's processes. They are their product, and their product is them!

CONCLUSION

Well, there you have it: the results of more than a year of traveling around the U.S., talking to great sales professionals, plus six months of hard pattern recognition.

You have probably noticed a couple of things. The first can be summed up with Shakespeare:

> There are more things in heaven and earth, Horatio,
> Than are dreamt of in your philosophy.
> — *The Tragedy of Hamlet, Prince of Denmark*

Prince Hamlet was a wordy fellow, and here he is saying that, indeed, maybe there are some new things out there you have yet to discover.

These 21 Secrets are the very core behaviors of the men and women at the top of their profession. When you apply these new ideas to your own career, you are guaranteed to build your skills and improve your performance.

When you picked up this book, it may have seemed almost

like a menu: a list of choices longer than the one at In-N-Out Burger, but way shorter than the one at the Cheesecake Factory. That's a really good way to look at the content. Here are twenty-one choices, twenty-one possible behaviors for you to work on to build your sales career. You will find some of these menu items very appealing and others about as appetizing as pineapple on pizza. (Okay, I realize many people, including my wife, find pineapple on pizza delicious. I am just not one of them.)

At Creative Ventures, we have taught the 21 Secrets to salespeople in many different industries. But never have we taught all twenty-one at the same time: That would just be too much information to incorporate into anybody's sales process at once. As you try to figure out which of these behaviors to implement first, you will find that some match your style and personality, while others don't. There are some that you can start immediately to gain a quick benefit. Others you will need to think about and implement more slowly. Some of the 21 Secrets may never fit your sales style. If you're truly at a loss for where to begin, I'll suggest again that you consider the Four Essential Secrets at the beginning of the book.

Start small. I can't imagine anyone who would dump their entire existing sales practice and embark on a new, twenty-one-part journey. Many of the salespeople we work with begin with—you guessed it—one to three new practices.

The second thing you've probably noticed can be summed up with scripture:

What has been will be again,
what has been done will be done again;
there is nothing new under the sun.

—*Ecclesiastes 1:9*

Yep, the Old Testament says it all: There are really no entirely new ideas. You may have thought, as you read some of these secrets, *Heck, I already know that. I probably don't* do *it, but I know that.* So here's hoping this book will inspire you to give some things a try.

That's how change happens. You come up with an inkling, a notion of *something*, and in order to give form to that something, you begin to look around. You find backup that gives your idea validity. If the concepts you find have been around for a while, with proven results, they become the bricks that support your idea.

"There is nothing new under the sun" is certainly true in business. You may think Henry Ford invented the assembly line. Well, not so much. You can trace the idea of linear assembly back to Colonial America, when Oliver Evans created the automated flour mill, and to the early 1800s in Hampshire, England, when the boys at the Portsmouth Block Mills created a mass production line to make the rigging blocks needed by the Royal Navy. Even in the auto industry it wasn't Ford who was first to the idea of the assembly line; it was Ransom E. Olds (yes, of Oldsmobile fame).

But Ford took the idea one important step further. He turned the assembly line into a *moving* assembly line. Ford did his research; he looked at all the other linear assembly setups out there and used his research to make a change.

None of the twenty-one patterns of behavior in this book is necessarily anything earth-shattering or universe-changing on its own. But every single person I interviewed, every million-dollar producer, did every single one of these twenty-one things in one way or another. The secrets may not all be new, but they are all important.

Finally, as you get to work applying this newfound knowledge to your career, remember that to get to where you want to be, start by assessing where you are now. When you're headed someplace using a global positioning system for guidance, the system starts by figuring out where you currently are. It does this by determining your latitude, longitude, and altitude. When using this book as your guide, you can determine the position I like to call your Now by assessing three things: your skills, your knowledge, and your expertise. Once you figure out your Now, you can then decide which of these elements to focus on in order to get where you would like to be.

SKILLS are the talents you bring to the job: clear communication, smart planning, organization, leadership, and so on. How are your skills? What do you need to work on?

KNOWLEDGE is the data that bounces around inside your brain: facts about the product or service you sell, the company for which you work, the industry in which your company competes, and the clients and potential clients you serve. How well do you know your stuff? Is knowledge an area you need to focus on?

CONCLUSION

EXPERIENCE is wisdom gained by doing: tagging along on calls with successful colleagues, attending meetings, and rehearsing scenarios to identify potential problems and find solutions. Are you new to your job? Could you use more hands-on experience?

There's nothing you—or I, or anyone—can do to change your Now. Your Now is what is. But you can change your position in the future by carefully assessing where you need improvement and applying the secret or secrets that will help you. This book is not about your Now; it's about where you're going, and how to get there.

I am honored that you gave time and intellectual effort to my book. Thanks.

And get to work!

ACKNOWLEDGMENTS

An author comes up with an idea. The author puts the idea to paper and figures out how the idea gains meaning and, hopefully, value to a reader, but that does not make a book. An actual published book is a group effort, and this small space is where the true picture gets to be revealed.

Thanks to Lynn Johnston, my agent. She used her insight and convinced me this idea was a book—a book she could sell—and I'll be damned, despite my skepticism, she was right.

All the people at Simon & Schuster/Touchstone who believed the idea was commercially viable and worked like hell to make it so. Cara Bedick, who took the manuscript and made it better. Michelle Howry, my original editor, who has moved on to other things but had an infectious enthusiasm for the book. Also Susan Moldow, David Falk, Tara Parsons, Shida Carr, Lara Blackman, Monica Oluwek, Nancy Tonik, and Cherlynne Li.

My editor, Lauren Lipton. I have written a lot of stuff over the years, but I wasn't a writer. Lauren taught me to be a writer and nurtured the idea to fruition. I hope this is only the beginning of our collaborations.

ACKNOWLEDGMENTS

My family: the love of my life, Laura, who released me to the Bat Cave to write and never once did anything but support the effort. She is my best critic and the smartest person I have ever known. My son Colin, who through his management of Creative Ventures gave me the gift of time. My son Dylan, who was always asking for updates. My mom, who after thirty-one years is still not sure what I really do for a living.

Friends like Big Dan, who gave me the greatest piece of writing advice I have ever received: "Write like you speak." Dr. Jim Hengstenberg, whose friendship and critical eye have made me better at what I do. C. Ryan, who for all the time he has known and worked with me never failed to remind me, "You should write a book."

Terri Snell, who opened the door by being the first to grant me access to many of the superstar salespeople who appear in these pages.

Every great salesperson who took time away from "eating what they kill" to teach me the key behaviors that make them million-dollar producers.

Anyone I might have missed: THANKS.

ABOUT THE AUTHOR

For more than thirty years, Stephen Harvill and his team at the boutique consultancy Creative Ventures have helped some of the world's most respected companies realize their true capabilities through implementing pioneering methods in organizational dynamics and strategic thinking.

Today Stephen works with organizations of all sizes to help them move past the boundaries and restrictive thinking that are pervasive across Corporate America.

As a respected educator, consultant, and strategist, Stephen works with companies to maximize the potential of their human capital and of the organization as a whole. Sometimes the changes are large, but often they begin with small, positive steps and creative approaches.

Stephen has applied the principles in *21 Secrets* to clients including IBM, General Mills, Wells Fargo, Pepsi, Southwest Airlines, Samsung, JCPenney, Microsoft, Apple, AIA, the US Navy, and Allianz.

His home base is in Austin, Texas, where he lives with his wife, Laura.

Printed in the USA
CPSIA information can be obtained
at www.ICGtesting.com
CBHW021435150524
8396CB00005B/16